THE
GHOST HUNTER
CHRONICLES

THE GHOST HUNTER CHRONICLES

Paul Keene, Gemma Bradley-Stevenson and Bryan Saunders

NEW HOLLAND

To Peter and Carol — without you this would have been impossible. Thank you for all you have done!

Haunted Britain were granted exclusive access to the Guild Halls of London featured in this publication. We have been extremely privileged to be invited to investigate these locations as they are not open to the public, and they have kindly allowed us to use our findings in our book. However, at their stipulation we have to inform all our readers that any future requests for admission to these premises will not be granted, so please do not attempt to contact them for this reason.

Thank you
Haunted Britain Team

First published in 2006 by New Holland Publishers (UK) Ltd

London • Cape Town • Sydney • Auckland

www.newhollandpublishers.com

Garfield House, 86-88 Edgware Road, London, W2 2EA, United Kingdom

80 McKenzie Street, Cape Town, 8001, South Africa

14 Aquatic Drive, Frenchs Forest, NSW 2086, Australia

218 Lake Road, Northcote, Auckland, New Zealand

ISBN 1 84537 267 0

Although the publishers have made every effort to ensure that information contained in this book was meticulously researched and correct at the time of going to press, they accept no responsibility for any inaccuracies, loss, injury or inconvenience sustained by any person using this book as reference.

Some of the photographs in this book have been enhanced, and do not necessarily portray actual apparitions.

Publishing Manager: Jo Hemmings

Senior Editor: Julie Delf

Assistant Editor: Kate Parker

Designer: Adam Morris

Production: Joan Woodroffe

Cartography: Bill Smuts

Reproduction by Pica Digital Pte Ltd

Printed and bound in Singapore by Kyodo Printing Co (Pte) Ltd

10 9 8 7 6 5 4 3 2 1

CONTENTS

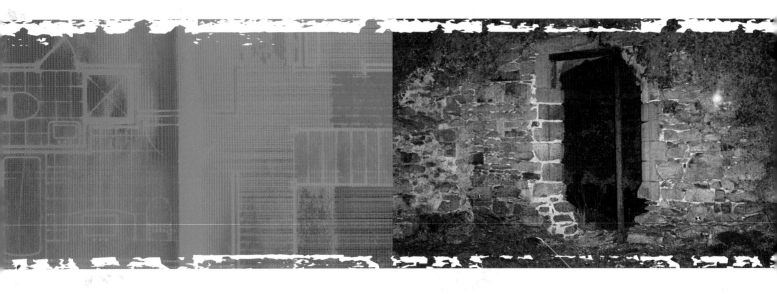

Investigations

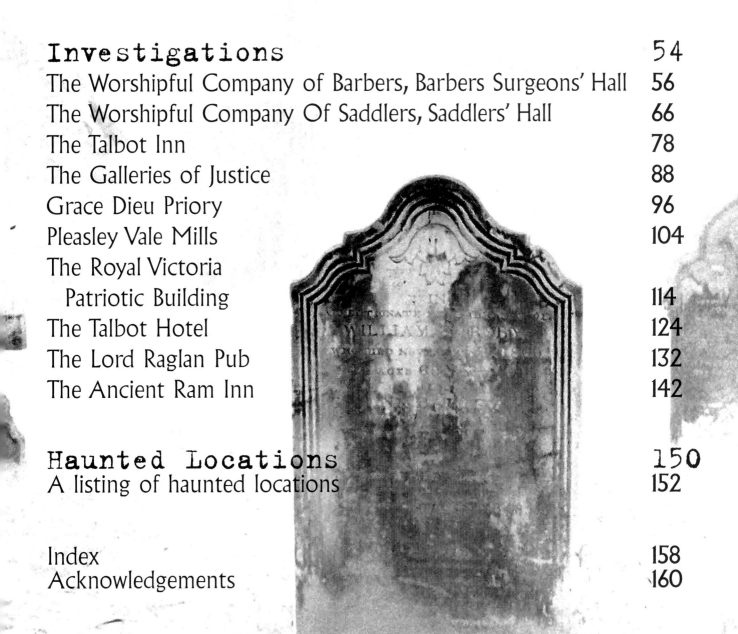

 FOREWORD

Ghosts – what are they, where do they come from and what, if anything, do they want with us mere mortals? These are the kind of questions that continually drive paranormal investigators on their quests to shed light on this very thought-provoking subject.

Ghosts, hauntings and all things paranormal have fascinated me from an early age, and the subject matter has almost been a lifelong companion. From my personal investigations, which started when I was in my late teens, to my more recent TV work, I have never tired of listening to accounts of ghostly goings-on, hearing about a new haunted location or reading the latest article or book on the subject.

Investigating ghosts is about as varied an occupation as you could possibly have, you never know what's going to happen from one location to the next – and that's one of the best things about it! But it does have its drawbacks: long hours and late nights – or maybe that should be early mornings – endless periods during which nothing happens, more of nothing happening and the loss of any feeling in your posterior while your fingers feel as if they're going to drop off from frostbite during a winter's investigation into a haunted ruin!

If that sounds like something you can put up with, great! If not then grab a warm drink, sit back and delve into this book – after all, someone else has done all the hard work!

Enjoy.

Phil Whyman
Paranormal Investigator
LivingTV's *Most Haunted* and *Scream Team*

INTRODUCTION

Welcome to *The Ghost Hunter Chronicles*, a detailed account of the investigations undertaken by 'Haunted Britain', an organization that first started researching the paranormal a long time ago. It has grown from a small group based in Leicester to an investigation team with five offices around the United Kingdom, and active members that include some of the most notable personalities in the paranormal field.

It's hard to believe that what started as a small group investigating dilapidated ruins in all weathers, has grown to an organization that is allowed unrivalled access to some of the country's most prestigious locations, including London's famous Guild Halls. So what can you expect from this book? Let me explain …

Of course, we wanted to create an account of our paranormal investigations and display our evidence for the world to see. However, our primary reason for writing *The Ghost Hunter Chronicles*, was to create a book aimed at those who want to start their own investigations into the paranormal world.

Our website receives hundreds of emails every month from people asking how they can start investigating ghosts and haunted locations and what they should do when they get there. If this is something you're thinking about, then this book is for you! And if you also want to see some amazing photographs of the paranormal in action – look no further!

Happy hunting!

Paul Keene
Co-founder, Haunted Britain
www.hauntedbritain.net

A GUIDE TO THE PARANORMAL

A good understanding of the paranormal is paramount when conducting investigations into ghosts and hauntings. The following sections detail some of the Haunted Britain techniques and methodology and are offered to help you with your own paranormal investigations. From questions of what is a ghost and spirit, to EMF Meters and Top Ten Tips, this section should shed some light on the most important side of paranormal investigations.

FREQUENTLY ASKED QUESTIONS

I WANT TO START GHOST HUNTING. WHAT ESSENTIALS DO I NEED?

You don't really need a great deal to go ghost hunting, but if you want to keep a record of your investigations you will need some equipment. Ideally you need a camera – digital models are great because of their clarity, quality and speed. A standard 35-mm camera is also OK, although the cost of developing could become astronomical, and your images may not capture anything other than scenery. Another worthwhile investment is a good video camera. This will help you to record events as they occur, including speech, which has been found to be of fundamental importance when hunting ghosts. A video camera will also be able to capture moving light anomalies (see page 23) and electronic voice phenomena, or EVP, (see pages 25–27). If possible, try to buy a camera that has night vision, or you won't be able to see anything that happens in the dark, which is when you are more likely to get the best footage. Video cameras also help to capture the atmosphere of your investigations for future viewing, although an open mind and enthusiasm are also essential to conduct this type of research. For more information on starting your own investigations, you can follow the various guides contained in this book.

WHY DID YOU START GHOST HUNTING?

Well, those involved in Haunted Britain have been interested in the subject for many years and always had a desire to find out whether ghosts exist, but didn't really know how to get started. Then television programmes such as *Most Haunted* and *Ghost Detectives* came along and showed that expensive equipment wasn't always essential – what was more important was the desire to get out there and do some ghost hunting. At first it was difficult for us to get access to sites to start our research, but once we had a few investigations under our belts, the doors of prospective sites began to open much more willingly.

BELOW *A locked off camera is set to record a haunted skittles table.*

TOP TEN TIPS

1. CONDUCT A PRELIMINARY INVESTIGATION AND ANALYSIS

As mentioned in our preliminary visit section (see page 17), conducting a visit prior to your investigation will garner better results.

2. ALWAYS CARRY SOME FORM OF IDENTIFICATION

It has been known, and is not uncommon, for paranormal investigators to be questioned by the police, villagers and local authorities during their investigations. We would also recommend that you have express permission, if needed, to conduct your investigation, and keep the documentation with you during your investigation.

3. CONDUCT YOUR INVESTIGATION BETWEEN THE HOURS OF 10PM AND 5AM

This may seem a bizarre tip, but it is recommended that you conduct your investigation between these times due to the common facts that most ghosts are seen at night and most people die during their sleep.

4. NEVER WEAR PERFUME OR AFTERSHAVE DURING YOUR INVESTIGATION

It is not uncommon for paranormal investigation groups to smell strange aromas during their investigations. By not wearing perfume or aftershave you are eliminating the possibility of false evidence occurring.

5. ALWAYS RESPECT YOUR LOCATIONS, AND, OF COURSE, THE DEAD

Paranormal investigation teams that gain access to haunted locations are very lucky. And it is *always* a good idea to be very respectful of the location. Please remember to clean up after yourselves, as it has been known for locations to ban further investigations because of the actions of some groups.

It is also important to be respectful to the dead. 'Ghost baiting' – where you deride the possibility of a spirit, swear or use other profane language or move objects that are revered in the location – is becoming increasingly common as a way to communicate, and is not a preferred method of objective investigation.

6. REMAIN OBJECTIVE DURING YOUR INVESTIGATION

The basis of an objective investigation is to question all possible phenomena before you decide they are of a paranormal nature. This includes getting professionals to look at photographs and allowing different people to view the evidence.

Only when there can be no other explanation for the phenomena can it be deemed paranormal.

7. BE AWARE OF THE AMOUNT OF INVESTIGATION THAT IS REQUIRED

Paranormal investigation is not only attending the investigation itself, but trudging through hour upon hour of locked off camera footage. On a normal investigation we obtain around 15 to 20 hours of footage and every second has to be analysed.

8. ALWAYS TAKE MORE BATTERIES THAN YOU COULD POSSIBLY NEED

It has been known for objects used during a paranormal investigation to cease to function during the investigation itself. The common school of thought on this topic is that if there are any spirits present, then they drain the power sources available to try and respond to any questions you may ask. However, this does not discount faulty batteries.

9. GLOW STICKS! GLOW STICKS! GLOW STICKS!

If you do reach a situation where your batteries have died, and you are left with no light – then it is recommended that you have a few glow sticks with you. These are chemical-based light sources and cannot be drained of power.

10. ALWAYS BE POLITE – THIS GOES FOR GHOSTS TOO!

Manners cost nothing. If the proprietor of a venue has allowed you access to a location then it is a great idea to write a letter of thanks, and also allow them the opportunity to sit in on your investigation. It is also highly recommended that you thank the spirits attempting to communicate with you.

LEFT *The Grace Dieu. Like many ruins, this location is renowned to be haunted. But as the posts suggest, safety is a big issue as the aging structure is slowly disintegrating.*

WHY ARE GHOST SIGHTINGS ONLY SEEN AT NIGHT?

In short, they're not. This is a common misconception, as hauntings and sightings of ghosts can occur at any time of the day or night. However, it is true that the majority are experienced after dark. It is thought that most people die between the hours of 2am and 6am, which is why most occurrences are recorded at night. This is only a theory, but it seems to be the most plausible explanation. There is also the issue of daylight (see below).

ARE GHOSTS ONLY VISIBLE IN THE DARK?

This is a difficult one! Technically, no, but it is true that the majority of footage captured of 'ghosts' and light anomalies is caught on cameras using night vision functions. However, we have caught light anomalies in the daytime on both video camera and digital still cameras. One explanation may be that ghosts consist of energy and often take the form of light anomalies, which means that they are more difficult to see with the naked eye if the surrounding light is good. Likewise, if you switch a light on in a room that is already lit by natural light, the extra light makes little difference and it isn't particularly noticeable. This may explain why ghosts and light anomalies are not often seen or detected during daylight hours, as a light in the dark is more easily illuminated and is going to be easier to see with the naked eye.

SHOULD I GO ON INVESTIGATIONS ON MY OWN?

No — for safety reasons this is a really bad idea. As a significant number of haunted sites are old, derelict or isolated, and investigations usually take place in the hours when most normal people are tucked up in bed, it is not a good idea to go ghost hunting alone, as accidents do happen. If you do, you must take a mobile phone with you and notify friends and relatives so that they know where you are and what you are doing. If anything does go wrong you can be contacted or found. Also, if you are on your own and you witness something paranormal, it is always wise to have the support of others. They may not have exactly the same experience, but they will be able to vouch for your state of mind and the circumstances surrounding the occurrences. Ideally, find a local group of ghost hunters or a few friends that you can trust and go ghost hunting safely.

I HAVE JUST STARTED A PARANORMAL GROUP, BUT WE DON'T HAVE A PSYCHIC OR MEDIUM. IS IT SOMETHING WE SHOULD ADVERTISE FOR?

No, not necessarily. Haunted Britain does not use psychics in its investigations, and it hasn't stopped us getting good results. In fact, the times that we have involved 'psychic mediums', we have recovered very little substantial evidence or none at all. One of our members is a 'sensitive', and can tune in to spirits, but she does not class herself as a medium. Sometimes having a psychic medium in a group can make you believe that something is there when it's not. We prefer to get solid physical evidence that can be viewed and scrutinized by everyone involved. Evidence put forward by psychics has to be received very cautiously, as not everyone can tune in to what they are experiencing. This sort of information can also be very suggestive. If a psychic medium indicates that they can see someone standing in the corner, you immediately start to feel uneasy simply because the suggestion has been made. This is not to say that psychics and mediums aren't a good idea in the right circumstances, but make sure that they can be trusted to give true and honest readings — there are many fraudulent individuals claiming to provide psychic services out there, so please be careful.

WHAT ARE 'COLD SPOTS'?

They are exactly as they sound — areas where the temperature drops dramatically, and the effects can be felt on the skin or recorded by infrared thermometers. They are usually attributed to spirits that are present or that want to make their presence known. Cold spots are usually accompanied by physical effects, such as the shivers or hairs standing up on end. When carrying out your research, however, ensure that there are no other factors that could influence or create the impression of unusual cold spots, for example draughts or open windows. This should be noted when you do your baseline tests (see page 51) before you start your investigation. Similarly, you can experience 'warm spots', which, unsurprisingly, are areas where an increase in temperature occurs. These are often thought to be the result of 'friendly' spirits being present. Sometimes warm or cold spots can affect an entire room or emanate from a certain point — be sure to ask others what they feel about the temperature rather than saying 'do you feel cold?' It eliminates the risk of being suggestive.

PRELIMINARY VISITS

If you are lucky enough to gain access to a haunted location (please see pages 152–157 for a selection of listings), then a preliminary visit is well worth the effort. This will allow you and your paranormal investigation group to get to grips with the layout of the venue and conduct initial baseline tests (see page 51). It will also allow you to assess whether there are any natural draughts or temperature changes at the site.

It is a good idea to ask the proprietor of the venue about the wiring, as your EMF Meter (see page 53) may well go off the scale if you are not forewarned about wiring hidden within the walls, ceiling and floor. Your preliminary visit is best conducted during the night, so you can attempt to replicate the conditions you will experience during your actual investigation.

It is recommended that you interview any witnesses to phenomena that have been reported at the site. By doing this, you will gain valuable information about the nature of the apparitions, what they do, where they come from, what they look like and where they go!

If you are visiting a pub or inn, then we would recommend asking the bar staff and landlord/landlady if visitors have witnessed anything inexplicable. We often find it is only when you start talking to people who live locally that a fuller explanation for possible ghosts becomes apparent.

If you are conducting an outdoor investigation, a preliminary visit during the daytime is also recommended, as you can document any obstacles that may hinder your investigation, such as bright street lamps, display lamps or wildlife. It is also recommended that you pay attention to the ground and make sure that you are fully aware of any bumps or stray pieces of stone.

And finally, we would strongly recommend you research the availability of parking on your preliminary visit. There is nothing worse than trudging through fields in the pouring rain to get to your desired location.

CAN GHOSTS HURT YOU?

If you ask the experts they will say 'no'. But it has been known for individuals to be hit, pushed, pinched or scratched. I suppose it depends on your personal pain threshold! Poltergeist activity (see pages 24–25) is more often attributed to people being hurt or injured. Our policy is safety in numbers – if you believe that there is the possibility of a situation turning nasty then do not enter in to it alone! Also, if you are in the dark, you are more likely to bump into things you can't see – so exercise caution. Don't run anywhere or enter areas that are not easily accessible. There may be times during paranormal investigations when you feel ill or physically sick. This can be spirits attempting to impress their feelings or conditions onto you, but it could also be claustrophobia, disorientation or even fear. Having experienced a ghost sighting myself, I can confirm that you are more likely to be emotionally and mentally wounded than physically.

HOW DO I KNOW WHAT IS SUBSTANTIAL EVIDENCE AND WHAT ISN'T?

Evidence is a difficult thing to prove when dealing with ghosts. There will always be someone who didn't witness the

BELOW *A locked off camera is aimed at a haunted painting which is said to watch you wherever you stand in the room.*

event who will put forward arguments to challenge the results you have collected. The secret is to be extra vigilant with regard to any external factors that could interfere with your investigation. Ensure that only you and your group have access to the areas you want to investigate and that they can be accounted for at all times. If you have trigger objects, aim cameras on these, ensuring that all angles and surrounding areas are visible. Take as many photos as you can using a selection of different cameras. If something is caught on more than one device, then it is less likely to be a technical fault. Also, be open-minded about what constitutes positive evidence and what can be assumed or dismissed. Think through every inevitability before offering your discoveries as 'proof' – if you can back up every possibility yourself, then you will appear more professional. For a guide to what makes good or poor evidence, see our information section (pages 38–53).

WHY DO ALL GHOSTS SEEM TO BE FROM A LONG TIME AGO?

There have been some reports of modern ghosts, but most sightings do involve spirits from centuries ago. It is a strange phenomena and one that nobody seems to have an answer for, although there are many theories and ideas as to why this appears to be the case. It may be because the majority of paranormal cases occur in old buildings or places of historical significance. Ghost hunters also rely on history

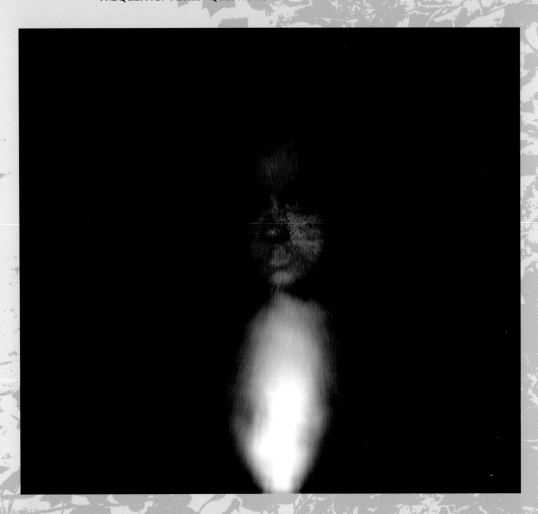

books for research, and urban myths and legends, which can last for centuries, passed down through each generation. It may be that cremation has an affect on the spirit, and most people today are cremated rather than buried. Perhaps it is the way in which a person dies that determines whether they become a ghost — most spirits appear to have come to a devastating or traumatic end or died suddenly. Despite what the modern media would have you believe, many more murders, lynchings, executions and fatal accidents occurred in previous centuries and most fatal ailments were due to a lack of hygiene and medical technology. Nobody will ever know exactly why there are more ancient spirits than modern, but these are a few theories to think about.

I THINK THAT MY HOUSE MAY BE HAUNTED? WHAT DO I DO?

This largely depends on how you feel about sharing your house with a spirit and also what form the entity takes on. If the presence of a ghost or the mere thought of your house being haunted is frightening, and you feel that you can not live there any longer, then you may need to seek help. You should consider contacting a recommended paranormal investigation group. They will speak to you in detail and take accounts from people who have felt, heard or seen something in the house. They will also want to visit your house and do some experiments to check for paranormal activity. They may want to visit more than once, or leave some equipment running to record activity over a longer period of time. Some groups have mediums as members or will at least be able to put you in touch with one. They can offer a little more detail about a spirit presence, as they claim to be able to contact the spirit through the power of the mind. From experience, those that request little or no money for their services are more likely to give a true reading. Unfortunately, there are many suspect psychics in the paranormal business. Be selective and if possible have more than one reading taken of your property. As with any business offering a service, make sure that they are well recommended and think carefully about handing over any payment.

WHAT IF MY HOUSE IS HAUNTED AND I WANT IT TO STOP?

If you are concerned that the entity is of an 'evil' nature, it is causing too much disruption or you simply don't like the thought of sharing your home with previous occupants who have passed on, then you may want to consider having the house blessed or cleared. Some mediums and psychics claim to be able to do this, but you should contact a local church for help and advice with this. Some churches will not entertain such practices, but keep searching, as someone somewhere will be able to offer a solution.

I AM BUYING AN OLD HOUSE OR BUILDING. HOW DO I FIND OUT IF THE PROPERTY IS HAUNTED?

There is currently no law stating that paranormal activity that has occurred in a property being purchased has to be declared. However, due to the rise in lawsuits against vendors who have not supplied such information, the law may have to be changed in the future. Some sellers think that paranormal experiences may devalue their property, as it would put many people off, which is why they choose not to disclose such information. If you are not concerned about the implications of living in a haunted house, make sure you express this to the vendor and he or she will probably be more open and willing to reveal any secrets about the property. Try doing some research of your own to see if there have been any reported hauntings. Old newspaper articles and neighbours are good places to start this sort of research.

Similarly, if you are trying to sell your house and you believe it is haunted don't be too worried that nobody will want to buy it. In one case in the USA, a property that proved difficult to sell was snapped up by two paranormal enthusiasts, after they went into the attic and had a 'spooky' encounter. The owners admitted that many people viewing the house had experienced the same thing and it had put them off buying the property. But for the couple concerned, it was the icing on the cake – they jumped at the opportunity to live there, offering the asking price within ten minutes of viewing. However, in such situations it's wise to exercise extreme caution, as you don't want another 'Amityville' situation on your hands.

HOW CAN I GAIN ACCESS TO HAUNTED LOCATIONS?

The paranormal investigation industry has sky-rocketed in recent years, and it's becoming a very lucrative sideline for many day-to-day businesses. It seems that if you want to get ahead in business, get a ghost. Hotels can charge higher rates for rooms that are renowned for paranormal sightings and activity. Likewise, many haunted inns, pubs and buildings are asking for large sums of money to hold overnight investigations. Haunted Britain started its investigations in some local public houses that had a lot of history attached to them and which had already experienced a few sightings.

We advise that you start with outdoor locations or smaller premises that are unlikely to be inundated with requests from ghost hunters. Start out by ringing around, ensuring that you sound authoritative and you are prepared for property owners to ask many questions. You are less likely to be successful if you hunt alone, so try and form some sort of group, even if the members are from your family. And try and have a name for your group, as it sounds more impressive.

The more locations you investigate, the easier it will be to get in to larger, more prestigious sites. The more well-known the location, the harder it will be to gain access. At Haunted Britain we wrote many letters to the sites of prospective investigations asking to do investigations and found that you receive very little response by way of return — but you have to keep trying. If you would like to research the famous locations, you may have to finance it yourself, which can be extremely expensive, running to several thousand pounds for just a few hours. To reduce costs you could try and gather your friends together to help share any fees, or you could go on an organized tour with an established group. But check first whether they will let you do your own investigating. Some groups will not let you undertake your own experiments and are more likely to hold staged events.

BELOW *Example of initial contact letter. It is worth writing to prospective locations in advance of a phone call. Perseverence is a must, as you are unlikely to get a response on your first attempt.*

Main Contact Name
Ghost Group Name
Address
Telephone
Fax
Email

To Whom This May Concern

Thank you for taking the time to read this letter. Permit me to introduce myself. I am [insert name] and I run the paranormal investigation group [group name].

Whilst conducting our research into haunted locations, we came across your esteemed venue and wondered about the possibility of conducting a scientific investigation into the paranormal.

The investigation team will consist of [X] members (including me) and we shall be held accountable for all damage to any property. We are also covered under our insurance for the sum of [insert insurance amount].

We would require access to your location for a period of three to five hours during the evening or night in order to conduct a series of scientific tests that will try to capture proof of the existence of the paranormal.

We will take every effort to conduct this investigation away from the view of the public so as not to arouse their interest. We will also inform the local police of our intentions, so as not to arouse any form of suspicion.

If possible, we would also like to visit your venue in the daytime to have a walk around and get our bearings and make notes of anything that could be construed as paranormal.

If you require any considerations to be met before an investigation takes place, please contact us as soon as possible so we can make all members of our investigation team aware.

[insert this following section where applicable]

We would invite you to stay with us during this investigation, as your knowledge of the building will prove both fascinating and insightful if we do encounter any form of paranormal activity.

Thank you once again, I hope to hear from you soon

Yours faithfully,

MY TOWN HAS A LOCAL 'GHOST WALK'. WHAT SHOULD I EXPECT?

Ghost walks are great fun, and on some occasions they can be quite hair-raising. They often involve a tour of historical sites in your local area, along with renditions of local folklore and ghostly goings-on. Some ghost walks take in public houses, so that those involved can sample a little Dutch courage along the way; others may start or finish with vigils at a haunted location. All such events are meant to provide entertainment, so don't expect to get any serious investigation done.

BELOW *Floor plans are an essential part of paranormal investigations. By using them you can keep notes on events and where they occurred. They can also prove to be a useful visual reference in searching for an explanation of any potential paranormal phenomena.*

WHAT DO I DO IF I THINK I MAY HAVE CAUGHT SOME EVIDENCE OF PARANORMAL ACTIVITY?

The first thing you should do is document it — write down everything that you can remember. Draw out a plan showing who was standing where when the paranormal activity occurred and record any strange feelings that were experienced at the time. Check through any video footage repeatedly, and analyse the event as logically as possible, examining whether there could be any natural cause for the anomalies that have occurred, such as light refraction, dust, moisture or the reflections from polished or shiny surfaces. If you have ruled out every possible factor, and are still convinced that you have experienced something paranormal, it may be worth sending your evidence to a professional for verification. Many websites, including Haunted Britain, have a facility that allows you to submit photographs and video footage. We will look at it for you objectively, and let you know what we find.

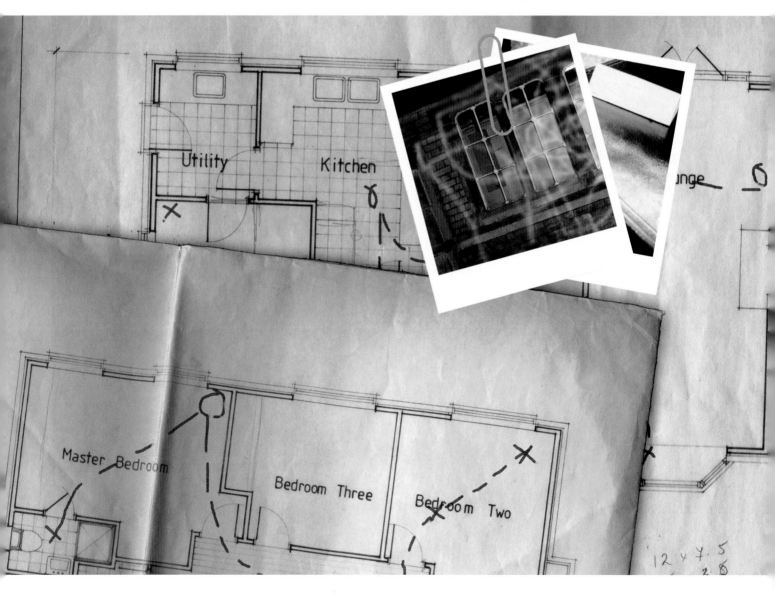

COMMON PARANORMAL EXPERIENCES

ORBS AND LIGHT ANOMALIES

'An orb is the first visible manifestation of a sentient spirit. Its shape is usually a globular or spherical ball of light, which moves at various speeds and in various directions. They are mostly white or translucent, although colouration is known. They range in size from small (1–2cm in diameter) to huge (20cm or more in diameter). They appear at all types of environment and in all kinds of weather conditions.'

Bryan Saunders, paranormal investigator

Orbs are a contentious issue within paranormal research at the moment – many are said to exist, but actual evidence is scant at best. Bryan Saunders' explanation is the current conventional paranormal description of these light anomalies. It seems simple enough, and would certainly explain why haunted locations play host to glowing balls of light that move about. These light forms also seem to shift on command or appear if called, which provides clear evidence that they are sentient. They appear to be made of energy, so they are energetic beings. Mobile orbs tend not to be viewed by the naked eye and appear to be filmed only by infrared or night-shot sourced video recorders. They are often caught on digital still cameras, although very rarely does the orb appear to be moving. Case closed. Or is it?

Here is a definition of an orb that gives a rational explanation for light anomalies, again by Bryan Saunders:

'An orb is a natural airborne object which reflects light back and is thus detected by anyone recording the immediate environment with a device which can record light. Its movement is either self–propelled, or due to air currents or ... gravity. Any occurrence of them moving or appearing on command is pure coincidence. Size variances occur due to the size of the object or proximity to a camera lens.'

Natural objects that reflect light in this manner include dust – the most commonly photographed 'orbs' are likely to be dust particles; small insects (although in Britain bioluminescent insects aren't common) and atmospheric moisture – rain or mist can easily account for most orbs captured outdoors and multiple orb photographs.

Presuming that the above statements are correct, orbs should be fairly prevalent at both haunted and not-so-haunted locations. There are, however, many problems with identifying paranormal orbs correctly. This has a lot to do with digital cameras and the way that they actually take a photograph.

THE STONE WALL PHENOMENA THEORY (SWPT)

The Stone Wall Phenomena Theory (SWPT) is a fairly simple idea and could, if it is correct, reveal two things – first, that there is a difference between ghosts and spirits (if they exist, see page 29), and second, some 'paranormal' phenomena may actually be very natural occurrences, but as yet unexplained or lacking investigation by 'conventional' scientific means.

The SWPT basically states that an environment can capture and record events that have affected that environment and that these events can be replayed to a perceptive or receptive

BELOW *The ancient walls of Grace Dieu Priory.*

ndividual. The easiest way to think about this is to imagine that the environment is a blank video cassette. An event is recorded onto this and is replayed at a later point. Some people can watch the tape, some people can't. That's easy enough. What we have a problem with is *how* the event is recorded and *how* it is replayed.

It is argued that all organic objects can absorb certain wavelengths of energy and radiation, and it stands to reason that they should also be able to radiate this energy. We certainly know that humans emit a weak electromagnetic field, so it follows that ghosts and spirits would too.

POLTERGEISTS

The word *poltergeist* comes from a German word that translates as 'noisy spirit'. There is a huge range of phenomena attached to poltergeists, including random objects being placed in a stack in the middle of a room or shelf, small fires breaking out, items appearing or disappearing, strange smells, peculiar noises, physical attacks and things being used against people, for example, flying knives!

Poltergeist hauntings have certain characteristics:

• They tend to start slowly and build up to a peak, before diminishing over a period of time or suddenly disappearing.
• Some poltergeist phenomena seem to defy logical thinking,

for example, one incident recorded a tall stack of sugar cubes appearing in a bathroom overnight!
• Poltergeist phenomena seem to focus on one or two specific individuals at a time, often young women who are just entering puberty.
• It appears that the victims of such phenomena are sometimes classed as 'sensitives' or 'mediums'.
• A poltergeist exorcism may or may not be successful — sometimes it makes things worse!
• The phenomena can and does happen at any time of day or night.

These examples only tell part of the poltergeist story, as there is some debate amongst researchers about what such a phenomenon actually is. There are two main schools of thought regarding these hauntings — the spirit and the non-spirit.

The first approach basically believes that the poltergeist is literally a noisy spirit, a discarnate intelligence that is, for whatever reasons, manifesting itself close to living people, while also producing odd and potentially dangerous phenomena. It can be dealt with and investigated by trained mediums, members of the clergy, irrespective of religion, and it is likely to disappear if an exorcism or rescue takes place.

The non-spirit approach comes from a very different perspective. It argues that much of the phenomena attributed to a poltergeist could be faked either consciously or

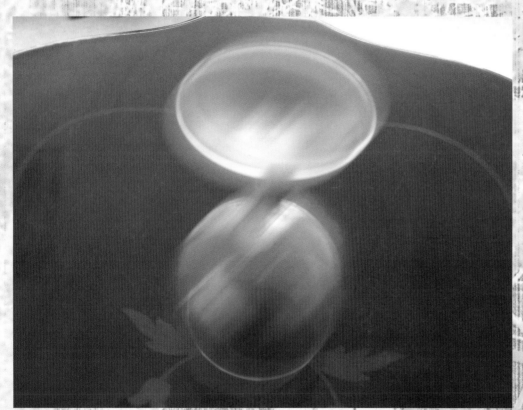

LEFT *Glass moving is a Victorian method of communication, spirits are said to channel their energies and communicate via movement.*

OPPOSITE *Table tipping is another Victorian method of communication. By lightly touching the table and allowing it to move, it is said that spirits can communicate with us.*

investigative teams to leave without witnessing something, and so imitates their poltergeist.

• The full-blown phenomena surrounding a poltergeist are occurring, but the victim is scared that the team may leave, so they contribute to the activity.

• The full-blown phenomena are occurring, but the victim wants more attention.

• The full-blown phenomena are occurring, but the victim is unaware that they are faking these actions.

ELECTRONIC VOICE PHENOMENA (EVP)

Electronic Voice Phenomena (EVP) is a blanket term that is used to describe any recorded sounds that are alleged to be paranormal in origin. A more accurate term used should be ASP – Anomalous Sound Phenomenon, as this includes bangs, knocks and other sounds, such as recording Second World War bombers flying over London in 2005!

In simple terms, an EVP is a recorded sound that was not audible while the recording was taking place. For example, two men are talking and a distinct female voice is heard to speak. The men in question know that there were no women present at the time of the recording, so where did the voice come from?

The Haunted Britain Team has defined the EVP in paranormal terms as:

'... the recorded voices of discarnate sentient spirits. They can leave messages, open conversation, ask questions or respond to questions asked out loud. The voices cannot be heard by the human ear, but can be heard as a recorded, compressed sound.'

However, although this description seems to leave no room for argument, there are many non-paranormal explanations for noises that may at first appear to be EVP:

• **Mobile phones** – not only do these devices give off radio waves that can be picked up by a tape recorder microphone, but you may also inadvertently pick up other conversations. If you are unaware that a mobile phone is being used near your recording device, then you could easily record it accidentally and believe the voices are EVP.

• **Radio waves** – radio broadcasts can easily be caught by a recording microphone and be confused as EVP. There are many legal and some illegal stations broadcasting all over the world and on many different frequencies. It stands to reason that some EVP are radio broadcasts.

subconsciously by the victim. Another non-spirit avenue explored to explain the phenomenon is psychokinesis, or PK for short.

It has been noted that a lot of this chaotic type of phenomena takes place around young pubescent or pre-pubescent individuals. Some researchers argue that the turmoil caused by the changes occurring in the body at this time creates huge amounts of stress, which is dealt with by the subconscious and unleashes huge bursts of psycho-kinetic energy. This manifests itself in all kinds of ways, but normally as objects being moved, hurled around or in other bizarre ways. As a result, some believe poltergeist activity is a *natural* rather than a *supernatural* phenomenon. This belief rests on the premise that psychokinetic energy is natural, but because it has not been proved that such energy exists it could still be argued that the phenomena surrounding suspected poltergeist activity is actually supernatural.

From the perspective of a paranormal investigator it has certainly been observed in several cases that poltergeist victims appear to have faked some of the phenomena relating to them, for example, blatantly banging water pipes or destroy-ing objects. Researchers who encounter this sort of behaviour have several avenues they can choose to believe or explore:

• The whole poltergeist phenomenon is fraudulent.

• Certain phenomena do occur, but the victim doesn't wish

These first two types of EVP interference are known as cross modulation.

• **Solar and interplanetary winds** – these can be recorded and sound *very* much like EVP. Yet they are a totally natural phenomenon. To hear sounds from the Sun, Jupiter and Saturn being caught on solar winds go to http://www.paravision.homestead.com/Level5.html. This website contains some very detailed analysis of the anatomy of an orb and explains how solar winds create a charge as they hit the Earth's magnetosphere, which resonates as sounds we can't hear but that can be recorded.

• **Reflected sounds** – every surface reflects sound and sometimes you can hear it echoing round a room. Some of these sounds can actually be reflected through walls or along corridors and eventually get picked up by recording devices and be mistaken for EVP. Reflected sound also applies to noises caused by plumbing!

• **Psychological mistakes** – the human mind is trained to recognize human sounds and noises from an early age, certainly from the second you are born and possibly in the womb. Consequently, an EVP that you think is saying 'Mummy' and can clearly be heard, could also be translated as 'money' or 'moan at me', among other things. This leads to a whole debate on EVP and how they are recorded (see opposite). More importantly it indicates ambiguity in the sound recorded. It is also worth noting that we hear sounds that resemble human voices because these are what we are most used to hearing! Therefore, a sound concealed in static or white noise may well be translated as a 'voice', when it is in fact nothing of the sort. This indicates that many EVP are not reliable as paranormal evidence. Work by Dr James Alcock, an eminent psychologist, has shown over and over again that people hear what they want to hear in static noise. His work cannot be underestimated, as it has been carried out under strict scientific control and has been proved to be correct. A good parallel for hearing 'hidden' paranormal sounds are the court cases of the 1980s, which levelled accusations of 'hidden messages' at the rock band Judas Priest and the solo artist Ozzy Osbourne. It was shown in court that these messages were natural pauses of breath, and that is was coincidental that they sounded like other words when played backwards. How many EVP could also fall into the same category?

• **Blatant fraud** — some people, for reasons known only to themselves, may try to invent paranormal phenomena. Fortunately, the Haunted Britain team has not come across this as yet. But during your own investigations, don't rule out hidden microphones, public address systems, tape recordings or hidden individuals you are unaware of! All of these should be fairly easy to investigate and rule out, and most cases of odd noises heard during your investigations that are not paranormal are likely to be non-fraudulent.

So a rational, scientific explanation for a sound initially identified as a paranormal EVP or ASP could be, as Bryan Saunders explains:

'A sound which cannot be immediately accounted for by a normal and logical cause but is most likely natural in origin.'

But science cannot always easily explain the strange noises captured during paranormal investigations. The Haunted Britain team has many examples of sounds that cannot be explained by any of the natural phenomena detailed above and so may be genuine EVP or ASP. Some seem to be recordings of human voices that are so loud that they drown out the person speaking — yet they don't match any of the voices of the investigative team. The team certainly has evidence of one EVP that was recorded when there was only one person in the room. The sound recorded was that of a very loud human voice saying a very clear and specific phrase — and the sound file needed no cleaning or clearing up. Only a minute or so later a sound was recorded which sounded like a human voice saying 'shhh!' very clearly and abruptly.

There are many problems with EVP recordings, however, several things are immediately apparent:

• They appear to be recorded anywhere, irrespective of whether a place is alleged to be haunted or not.
• They seem to be recorded in various countries around the world.
• They appear to be recorded in any conceivable language.
• They are recorded by people irrespective of age, sex, colour, religion, sexuality, education or economic status.
• They can be recorded irrespective of the cost of equipment — a cheap dictaphone is just as efficient as a mobile recording desk with an expensive microphone.

• Such sounds appear to be very short in length.

How are EVP recorded?

There are several methods of recording EVP (see the 'Experiments' section, pages 38–49), but the simplest method is to turn on a dictaphone or tape recorder and let it record. You can also detune a television set or radio and record the resultant white noise.

Because it is argued that spirits are made of energy, it follows that they can affect the energy that surrounds them. As all things are made of energy it should be relatively simple for a paranormal being to leave an imprint of its energy on a suitable recording material, for example, a magnetic tape. Consequently, a message is heard as the tape is replayed and a human ear hears the 'voice'.

BELOW *The Haunted Britain team set up for their overnight investigation.*

GHOSTS AND SPIRITS

Ghosts and spirits are initially confused by most people, as they are often believed to be the same thing — a discarnate energy that was formerly a human being or an animal. However, they are two totally different types of entity, and one is likely to be linked to the Stone Wall Phenomena Theory, or SWPT, (see pages 23–24). Let's start with a paranormal definition for a ghost:

> 'A ghost is a trapped entity which for some reason is caught up on Earth and forced to do the same thing over and over again. They can be helped by mediums who send them "into the light" or at least move them onto their next stage of existence.'

This in itself seems a fairly straightforward definition — until you consider a paranormal definition for a spirit:

> 'A spirit is a sentient energy which, for whatever reason[s], is either visiting or trapped on Earth. They sometimes appear to do the same thing over and over again, but most of the time they do their own thing. They can, if they want it, be helped by mediums who send them "into the light" or at least move them onto their next stage of existence.'

Again that seems simple enough. But what is the difference? Two things really: spirits are sentient, ghosts are not, and ghosts are not spirits — they are simply replays of previous events. The fundamental difference is the first — sentience. A spirit can interact within the environment in which it is present, a ghost cannot.

For example, a ghost of a monk walks through a wall, along a corridor and into another room. It does this every day at 5pm. As a paranormal investigator you have filmed this event, taken baseline readings for the area, conducted several light experiments and taken EVP readings. You decide to investigate what happens if you stand in front of the monk and you discover two things — either the monk walks straight through you or the ghost disappears the second it touches you. Absolutely no sentient interaction takes place.

Compare this to the behaviour of a spirit. The spirit of a monk walks through a wall, along a corridor and into another room. It does this everyday at 5pm. As an investigator you have filmed this event, taken baseline readings for the area, conducted several light experiments and taken EVP readings. You decide to investigate what happens if you stand in front of the monk and discover the following — the monk stops and moves around you! The following day the monk stops, looks at you and then moves around you. The day after that, the monk stops, looks at you, attempts to speak to you and then moves around you. The next day the monk simply ignores you and walks through you, but doesn't disappear. This indicates that the entity is capable of interaction with its environment - or sentience.

TYPES OF HAUNTING

Hauntings can be classified into several different types:

RESIDUAL HAUNTINGS

This type of haunting that is very likely to follow the form of the Stone Wall Phenomena Theory (SWPT) (see pages 23–24). Psychics and mediums refer to the SWPT as 'residual' because it exists as a remnant of events that happened, rather than a complete occurrence. Occasionally information is extrapolated from a residual experience, such as names and dates. The haunting itself may or may not be a regular occurrence.

GROUNDED HAUNTINGS

These hauntings are caused by spirits that seem to be linked to a specific place or, occasionally, an individual. The reasons a spirit may haunt in this manner are varied. The spirit may be guarding an area from intruders, as is the case with the room in front of the King's Bed Chamber at Tutbury Castle, Derby, which is still protected by the spirit of one of the King's Guard – occasionally he even becomes a little belligerent. A grounded spirit may be the victim of a murder, for example, London's Drury Lane Theatre is home to an apparition of this type. Another reason for this sort of haunting is that the subject is scared to go 'into the light', as is the case with the ghost of Mary, who haunts the Talbot Inn (see pages 78–87). These are just a few reasons why grounded hauntings occur, and there could be many more.

Psychics and mediums are often able to have conversations with the spirits involved in these sorts of events and can often ascertain why they are grounded. Once the reason for the grounding is known and has been dealt with, the haunting may stop.

VISITATION HAUNTINGS

A visitation haunting involves a spirit that comes and goes as it pleases. They can communicate with psychics and investigators alike and can manifest themselves fully, as and when they desire. These spirits have the capacity to completely

LEFT *One of the haunted suites at the Talbot Hotel – many different types of phenomena have been witnessed in this room.*

OPPOSITE *Clocks and watches have been known to stop or chime on the exact time when a person has died. While most occurrences are mere coincidence, others cannot be explained.*

interact with their environment, and they tend to visit
places they enjoyed in their
lifetime or people that they
knew and liked.

As is the case with
grounded spirits, there are
many reasons why this type
of haunting occurs, but a
very common reason is so
that the person now in spirit
form can comfort those who
are struggling to deal with
their loss. For example, a child
is so overcome by grief on
the death of a parent that the
parent returns to visit the
child and assure them that all
is well on 'the other side'.

A visitation haunting is
either the hardest type to
investigate or the easiest,
depending on the spirit's level

of interaction with its environment. If the spirit is present and
wants to command attention, it is able to do so quite easily. If
it is present but doesn't want to interact, then there's little that
can be done to encourage it, other than engaging in some
polite coaxing. The Haunted Britain team does not condone the
tactic of 'ghost baiting', which is the practice of annoying or
insulting a spirit in order to produce results. As a spirit of this
type can come and go as it pleases, there's every chance that it
will not be present when you attempt to investigate, and no
phenomena will be recorded or observed. Unfortunately, that's
how many paranormal investigations end up!

CRISIS APPARITIONS

A haunting of this type is very rare, lasting only a few seconds
– maybe a minute at best. As the name suggests, they are called
crisis apparitions because they occur at a moment of crisis, usually as someone is dying or about to die.

The current thinking surrounding these apparitions is that,
as a person dies, they instantly project their thoughts or their
spirit to their nearest and dearest in a final attempt to say good-
bye. The recipient of an apparition like this may see the person
walk into a room, hear them knock on a door or even have
them appear next to them while doing something mundane,
such as travelling on a bus! Most crisis apparitions occur in
cases of sudden death, for example a fatal accident.

Another commonly reported aspect of the crisis apparition
is that the time at which the phenomenon was experienced
tends to closely match the time of death or the time at which
the fatal incident happened.

POLTERGEISTS

See pages 24–25 for a detailed examination of this type of
haunting.

CYCLIC HAUNTINGS

These are hauntings that are alleged to happen at a specific and
regular time or date. They are fairly simple to identify and once
you have established the type of haunting that is occurring
then you can tailor any investigation accordingly.

It is believed that cyclic hauntings can involve multiple
events, so you may occasionally come across a residual
haunting alongside a grounded haunting. Sometimes these two
incidents are connected, for example a murder may well have a
residual replay, while the main protagonists of the event may
manifest themselves as grounded spirits trying to resolve the
situation in a different part of the investigation area.

Irrespective of the type of haunting, any investigations
about the subject should be carried out calmly, methodically
and professionally.

HOW TO CONDUCT A GHOST HUNT

Parapsychology — the scientific study of phenomena that are thought to have a supernatural origin — and paranormal research have always been dogged by accusations of sensationalism, fraud and wonderful phrases such as 'crackpot science' and 'its all occult / the work of the devil' and 'you're going to Hell!' For much of the time, the media hardly helps — the movie *Ghostbusters*, although a fantastic comedy, did more, in my opinion, to damage parapsychology than any other film dealing with 'the paranormal'. Current television coverage is not ideal — the notorious 1980s' BBC docudrama *Ghost Watch* glamorized and exploited a famous and particularly frightening case involving a poltergeist.

So how do you go about your own ghost hunting investigations properly and scientifically?

SETTING OBJECTIVES

Objectives are perhaps the most important part of any investigation and before you begin you must ask yourself what your investigation is setting out to achieve. When the Haunted Britain team starts an investigation we list our objectives as follows:

1. TO ASSESS WHAT, IF ANY, ALLEGED PARANORMAL ACTIVITY IS PRESENT AT THE INVESTIGATION LOCATION.

This is a simple point and it is fundamental to any form of paranormal investigation that is conducted, whether you are part of a huge professional team using lots of scientific equipment, 'sensitives' and mediums or just checking out the local cemetery with a couple of curious friends. Note the word 'assess' — you must aim to make an informed and unbiased judgement when you reach the end of your investigation. Is there any firm evidence of paranormal activity or can any incidents that occurred be explained as rational, normal phenomena that obey scientific laws?

2. TO ATTEMPT TO RECORD ANY EVIDENCE OF ALLEGED PARANORMAL ACTIVITY AS OBJECTIVELY AS POSSIBLE, UTILIZING SCIENTIFIC EQUIPMENT AND METHODS.

This is easier said than done — there is very little hard evidence in the public domain to support the belief that any form of paranormal activity exists. What we try to do at Haunted Britain is to record anything anomalous and assess objectively whether it can be explained from a scientific point of view. If it can't then it *could* be described as paranormal.

3. TO ASSESS ANY RESULTS ACHIEVED CRITICALLY AND EXPLAIN THEM FROM A NON-PARANORMAL PERSPECTIVE BEFORE TAKING A PARANORMAL PERSPECTIVE.

Let's face it, most of what we think of as paranormal phenomena can — and should — be explained as rational, normal, everyday occurrences. What are often thought to be orbs are usually specks of dust that have caught the light; that strange knocking is probably a dodgy pipe; the creaks you can hear are the floorboards or the house adjusting to environmental conditions. However, not every incident can be so easily explained or conveniently pigeonholed, and this is the phenomenon that needs the most consideration during any investigation or report into the paranormal. Even if a specific phenomenon is suspected as being paranormal, always point out that there could also be a rational explanation to explain the event — even if you don't believe this yourself. In these situations, you can always state that what has occurred is likely to have a rational explanation, but illuminate the points that may be paranormal — so that you have provided both a rational and a paranormal explanation if required.

4. TO ASSESS IF FURTHER VISITS ARE NEEDED TO INVESTIGATE THE SITE PROPERLY.

Some areas of suspected paranormal activity are considerably more active or larger than others and these may well require more than one visit to complete a satisfactory investigation.

5. To write up and publish (usually electronically) a critical report of the investigation, complete with supporting evidence and unbiased conclusions.

The publication of paranormal investigations serves several purposes: first it allows others to see your methodology; second it allows others to see your conclusions and third it allows others to appraise your findings and evidence. It also ensures that 'parapsychology' appears to be a valid scientific subject if researchers publish their findings.

Electronic publication is preferable to paper media, as you can contain moving images and sounds that can normally only be reproduced on disk or tape. And, of course, electronic publication is a little more environmentally friendly! Last but not least, publication makes a formal contribution to the evidence being gathered by groups around the world, which also reveals any patterns that arise from the use of specific methods.

Anthropology, Sociology & Cultural Considerations

In the UK we are extremely lucky to have a hugely diverse range of people and cultures, thriving in a tolerant society. Amazingly enough, this is something that can traced back for centuries.

BRIEFINGS AND TIMETABLES

A brief is very simple to do – it's just a quick talk about the areas that are to be investigated.

Timetabling your investigation isn't really that important, but it does help things run a bit more smoothly if everyone knows what they are doing, where they are doing it, when they are doing it and who they are doing it with.

There are several ways of writing a timetable for an investigation, but what is essential is that everyone has a copy not only of what their team is doing, but, if relevant, what other teams are doing.

It is VERY important that the investigation co-ordinator knows where everyone is supposed to be and when. This is a basic health and safety issue. For example, if team A doesn't get back to the base when they are due, then someone needs to find them and make sure they are OK – they may have had an accident and be out of radio contact. Or they could be actively recording the most fantastic phenomena ever – and you wouldn't want to miss out, now would you?

01.35 taking a baseline EMF reading

It can be shown that people emigrated to Britain even before the Romans arrived. Archaeological evidence from Stonehenge indicates that a united and established Europe-wide religious culture had existed since the Bronze Age, about 1,000 years before the birth of Christ — possibly even earlier. When the Romans invaded some 2,000 years ago, they brought with them people from different cultures who integrated with those already living here. Individuals from many different races and religions have been coming to these shores ever since. In short, the United Kingdom is rich in many different cultures and has been for thousands of years. But what does such diversity throughout history have to do with investigating the paranormal? The answer is, quite a lot!

Here is a typical — but fictional — example of an investigation into a haunted 16th-century building. The ghost of a murdered servant girl who was buried in a makeshift grave beneath the cellar floor has been seen roaming the building's wine cellar. This apparition is scaring the residents, who have asked a paranormal team to investigate.

The team perform all their preliminary checks — they have done plenty of research, including scouring parish and archaeological records and registers of births and deaths. As a result of their research, they have come up with a likely subject — Sarah Smith.

The team is all male.

Among the team is a competent medium, who establishes an impression of the murder while walking around the building and also comes up with the name of the person who committed the crime. The team set up trigger objects (see pages 47–48) — an Anglican crucifix, a coin taken from one of their pockets and a porcelain doll. The investigation is set up professionally and the equipment used includes multiple camcorders, tape recorders, dictaphones and digital EMF Meters.

The team now decide to attempt some communication and recite the following words out loud:

'If the spirit of Sarah Smith is present please come forward and communicate with us. You can do this by making banging sounds, manifesting as a light or speaking to our cameras or tape recorders. If Sarah Smith is not with us, then any other spirit is invited to do the same. We respect your presence and mean you no harm — we only wish to seek acknowledgement of your existence.'

The investigative team waits patiently for an hour and, as far as they are aware, no results are forthcoming. They move to another part of the building where the apparition has also been seen and repeat the process. A duplicate set of equipment is already set up at this site to save time. Again they wait patiently, but there are no visible or audible results.

The team splits into two to cover different areas of the building more efficiently. They continue their investigations for several hours, but neither group gets any results. The team eventually pack up their equipment. However, they are not completely disheartened, because they have not yet studied their recorded footage. But it's the same story and they are disappointed to find absolutely nothing on the recorded material — no sounds, lights, orbs or manifestations. Absolutely nothing.

This is a fairly typical result for many ghost-hunting groups up and down the country, but it is worth remembering that the nature of most paranormal phenomena is spontaneous and you may or may not always be able to capture it.

However, let's look at this example from a different perspective — that of the spirit. First, she is a murder victim — and she was killed by a man. The investigative team is all male. If she is sentient, she may well choose not to appear in front of a group of males simply because they terrify her.

Second, she can see no reason to approach the objects that they have placed out for her to examine — she is a Catholic, so although the crucifix is interesting it is irrelevant to her. The coin is modern and features the portrait of Elizabeth II — the spirit has no idea who this is, and although it confirms to her that she is dead, it does not connect her to her past. The final object, the porcelain doll, does not appeal to her as she is a woman, not a child.

Third, she knows these men are trying to communicate with her, and although they say they mean no harm, she is still too scared to talk. She could trust them more if another woman was present. Fourth, they are using very strange language. What is a camera? What is a tape recorder?

So from the spirit's point of view it is unlikely that she would want to talk or do anything the team desires of her because they are not considering *her* perspective. Her cultural context is firmly rooted in the 16th century — the investigators are using the cultural boundaries of the 21st century. The two worlds have very little in common.

The Haunted Britain team seem to get consistent results on our investigations because we take cultural and historical perspectives into account. What follows is a checklist of historical, social and cultural matters to consider when ghost hunting.

OPPOSITE *Baseline tests are an integral part of any paranormal investigation, use as many different pieces of equipment as possible to gather as much information as possible.*

RIGHT *Conducting the right research before and after your investigation is a priority. Make use of local libraries and record offices to help to quantify the paranormal phenomena.*

LANGUAGE

This is an extremely important consideration. Using the correct terminology is essential. Talking about modern technology while appealing to a spirit that hails from a distant historical period is pointless – the chances are they won't have a clue what you are talking about. Instead of using modern technological terms, try telling the spirits that you have objects in the room that can hear the words they speak and can see them. Assure the spirit that you will hear and/or see them eventually even if you cannot hear and/or see them now. The actual names of the machines become irrelevant – a sentient spirit will see them and it knows that it can communicate, even if it doesn't understand how the modern technology works. The Haunted Britain team adopts this approach and has often come away from an investigation with either EVP or ASP. Talk to spirits so that they understand what you are saying and what you are asking them to do when you are attempting to communicate.

The other thing to consider is what language the spirit spoke in their lifetime. For example, if you go to a haunted site and your research indicates that the spirit is a Spanish child, there is little point in trying to communicate in English.

AGE

This is another very important matter to consider. Is the spirit an adult or a child? If it is a child, then you need to address it as such. Does your group include a parent or a teacher? If it does, let them address the spirit and they may yield better results. A parent or a teacher is likely to be used to dealing with shy, playful or mischievous children.

RELIGION

Religion is a very important matter to take into account when you are attempting to contact any form of spirit, especially when using religious trigger objects. Using a Christian cross will not be much use if the supposed ghost was of the Jewish faith. It is also important to note that many religions do not believe in ghosts.

REASON FOR DEATH

The reason for death is another important factor to consider when you try and contact a spirit or a paranormal entity. If the person was killed by three men, then it follows that it is not a good idea to investigate with an all-male team.

LEFT *Make sure you and your team are fully aware of electrical points before your investigation. Otherwise you could end up with abnormally high EMF readings.*

ABOVE *The open ancient grave at The Ancient Ram Inn. Recent reports indicate that this is a burial site of sacrificial victims.*

EXPERIMENTS

Whether or not you have decided to use a medium or a sensitive to communicate with spirits, there are several experiments that you can also try, which could gain a response or a reaction. Here a few that the Haunted Britain team uses:

- Coloured lights (see page 39)
- Scrying (see pages 40–41)
- Powder-surface experiment (see pages 42–43)
- Double tape recording (see pages 44–45)
- Ouija board (see pages 45–46)
- Automatic writing planchette
- Animals
- Music response
- Period costume
- Table tipping
- Trigger objects (see pages 47–48)
- False Orbs
- Zener Cards
- Ionized atmosphere

The team always tries to carry out more than one experiment at a location, as if one fails or has limited results, another may be immensely successful. Most of the experiments listed can be used to attempt communication with spirits.

Recording the results of experiments is also important, even those that appear to have failed. The data compiled indicates how you have conducted an experiment, the results gained and whether any specific experiment was more successful than another. Here are detailed guidelines to some of the methods listed above.

BELOW *Trigger objects are essential to a paranormal investigation. Always remember to use items which have a link to the ghost or spirit.*

OPPOSITE *Torches are an essential piece of ghost hunting kit. Most investigations take place in the dark... so you'll need one to see where you're going. Never conduct a paranormal investigation without one per person.*

Coloured lights

This is a very simple experiment in which gels or bulbs are used to tint the surrounding area a specific colour. This sort of experiment has also been used historically – the Victorian Spiritualist movement used red lights when carrying out paranormal investigations, as it was thought to be conducive to spiritual activity. From a psychological perspective, red light tends to make you more alert and aware of your surroundings, which is probably why the military and other services use lights of this colour in emergencies.

The first decision you need to make is whether to use coloured bulbs or gels, which offer more flexibility. Many light bulbs are not available in more than a few colours, while gels are available in a multitude of various colours and shades. However, if it is more convenient, most hardware shops usually have a few different coloured bulbs in stock and nearly all carry red. Gels usually need to have to be ordered from specialist shops, such as model shops or

theatrical suppliers. To set up an experiment using coloured lights, beg, borrow or buy some desk lamps, preferably those with flexible necks. Make sure the plugs are fused and work properly. Now either replace the bulb with a coloured source or attach the gel to the front of the bulb casing. When you turn on the light the surrounding area will be bathed in a different colour. Be aware though that gels may well burn out before a bulb blows depending on length of use.

You can now conduct your vigil or attempt communication with your spirit illuminated by your chosen colour and record any phenomena in the normal way.

One advantage of filming with a night infrared source camera while using a red light is that your images will come out crystal clear and the range of the camera seems extended. This is because the light source is brighter than the camera's infrared source and it picks up the reflection of the coloured light. The Haunted Britain team does not recommend that you attempt infrared filming in normal daylight or bright light conditions.

SCRYING

Scrying is an ancient technique and has been used by many different cultures throughout the world. The premise is very simple – stare into a reflective surface and see what stares back!

There are several ways to scry, but the method explained here uses mirrors. Any reflective surface can be used to scry, certainly the ancients used special pools of water or oil. This is an experiment that should be done by a single investigator, while out of earshot of the rest of the team. However, this does not mean you should be out of shouting range of another individual – you may need urgent help if you suddenly become scared or if you see something belligerent enough to make you run – straight into a chair, door, microwave detector or camera arrangement.

The main reason why you should be isolated while scrying is so that your words don't influence anyone else who is gazing into the scrying surface.

This experiment can be done under any kind of lighting set up – the brightness of the light is not an issue, unless it is distracting. However, the Haunted Britain team prefer to perform scrying experiments in the dark. Here's how to set up this experiment.

1. Set up a mirror that can easily be viewed – a square or rectangular shaving mirror is ideal. The size is not important – it really depends on how far you have to transport it.

2. Set up a dictaphone or tape recorder to record what you are saying. This may also pick up EVP.

3. Set up a camera to film yourself and the scrying surface. Make sure that you don't have any lens flare that could be recorded – this could be interpreted as an unusual phenomenon.

4. Take a set of baseline readings before you start the experiment. Concentrate on the scrying surface and on yourself.

Take standard EMF, humidity and temperature readings for both.

5. Relax! This is easier said than done, although some simple meditation techniques can help.

6. Describe out loud what you are seeing and how you feel – even if you can only see your own face and feel nothing out of the ordinary. It has been known for people to see faces, darkness, tunnels of light, apparitions and other things. A word of warning – sometimes the things seen during this type of experiment are not always pleasant or expected!

7. Record a second set of baselines.

8. Record your experiment in the normal fashion and decide whether you need to repeat it again at another point or whether somebody else needs to attempt it.

There are several reasons why scrying may work, the most obvious of which is that the mind starts to play tricks on itself once eyes become tired from staring in a constant place. Alternatively, electromagnetic forces present in the area or infrasound (sound that is below the normal audible level) are known to cause the brain to hallucinate both visually and aurally.

If you see light anomalies, which can be discounted as having a natural origin, then you may be viewing a paranormal occurrence. It must be noted that the Haunted Britain team know of several cases where a spirit has only been viewed in a mirror. Should you view a suspected spirit in a mirror, you must resist the urge to spin around quickly to face it – these apparitions are gone in the blink of an eye. Try instead to watch what the spirit is doing and note down the time it appeared and disappeared as soon as you can. This may help you to see the phenomena again.

BELOW *Darkened rooms and back-lighting from equipment can cause mysterious shadows. Make sure you know where all your team members are, as their movement can often be mistaken for paranormal shadows.*

POWDER-SURFACE EXPERIMENT

This is another cheap and simple experiment that can yield some very interesting and positive results – it can also be used as a way of sealing off large, open areas if needed. The method is simple – take a large volume of talcum powder or chalk dust and cover your chosen surfaces with it. The premise of the experiment is that things interfering with or moving through the powdered area will leave an impression or a trail. Here's how to do it:

1. Choose your powder – the Haunted Britain team prefer talc because it is already ground to a very fine degree. If no talc or chalk is available then you can try icing sugar or flour.

2. Choose the area or surface where you wish to experiment. The ideal sites are surfaces or rooms associated with the spirit. However, you can try areas or surfaces where nothing paranormal has been seen just to see if anything happens.

ABOVE *Powder is placed around the area in which a ghost is meant to walk. A locked off camera is then trained on the vicinity and the area is left alone for the investigation.*

3. Record baseline readings for the area – EMF, humidity, temperature and, if possible, wind speed. Check the site thoroughly for draughts and eliminate them if required.

4. Set up cameras and dictaphones. Start recording *before* you dust the area, otherwise you may disturb the powder when you turn them on.

5. Dust the area and surfaces with the powder.

6. Using a portable camera, take photographs of the undisturbed dust. If any of the dust has been accidentally disturbed take photographs of that also.

7. Inform your fellow investigators that the areas have been 'dusted' and tell them not to go near them. If you have

animals with you, you may wish to remove them from the area or control their movements.

8. Now it's a simple matter of waiting until the end of the vigil or investigation when you record your results. Be *very* careful when assessing any disruption to the powder – you don't want to move dust accidentally and misinterpret it as paranormal.

9. Photograph the area again and any powder disruption – it is not unknown for handprints to be outlined in powder or possible writing.

10. Take another set of baseline readings.

11. Clear up any mess only after you are absolutely sure that you have recorded any phenomena caused by the experiment. Remember that once you have disturbed the powder there is no going back!

12. Record the experiment and its outcome in the normal fashion.

You can use the powder experiment in conjunction with experiments involving trigger objects. If an object is moved or has been examined then the powder is likely to be disturbed. This type of experiment is also very effective if you think someone is creating fraudulent phenomena and passing them off as supernatural – powder the areas on the floor where the 'phenomena' are happening and make up an excuse so that no investigator enters the site, but don't let the suspects know it has been dusted. If anything curious happens check the dust – shoe prints will inevitably be present and dust is likely to be present on the suspect(s). At this point inform the team that there may have been some interference with the experiments conducted. Pack your equipment and leave – politely, of course.

Remember that you are responsible for any mess caused and these sorts of experiments have the potential to be very untidy. Bring a small vacuum cleaner or a dustpan and brush so that you can clear up after yourself.

BELOW *Strange marks have been known to appear in powder experiments, such as this fragment of a hand print, asking the question – are they of paranormal origin?*

DOUBLE TAPE RECORDING

Tape recorders or dictaphones are essential pieces of equipment on any paranormal investigation. Using two or more at a time will help to verify any EVP that may turn up. It is helpful if both recorders are the same model and that they include tape counters, as this means your recordings and measurements will be consistent. As with most of the experiments, this one is very simple.

1. Set up recorder A at the site being investigated.

2. Set up recorder B on a parallel setting no more than 6 feet away from machine A.

3. Turn on both recorders and start recording. Record the location, time (preferably using the 24-hour clock), state who is in the room and where they are situated.

4. Conduct the investigation in the normal fashion.

5. Change tapes as and when required.

6. Listen to the recording from machine A and note down any suspected EVP or ASP. Note the number on the counter.

ABOVE *Dictaphones with an external microphone are a fantastic piece of equipment and can enable you to capture EVP without the enormous expense.*

7. Do exactly the same with machine B.

8. Compare any unusual sounds on the tapes and see if they have been duplicated. If you have a sound recorded on both tapes then it may well be a genuine EVP or ASP.

9. Analyse each sound using computer software and write up a report, including the frequency of each sound.

10. Archive the tapes.

You can try this experiment with multiple recording devices to compare results. The Haunted Britain team has had many successful results with this experiment. We sometimes use extra microphones on our recording devices, although we have not really noticed much of a difference in these cases except that you don't get as much hissing or the sound of the motor turning the tape. This may be significant in the cases of very quiet EVP or ASP, but for the most part these sounds should be loud enough to hear with the naked ear when a recording is played back.

One important final note – if you leave the recorders unattended and you need to go back into the area always announce that you're re-entering the site! This will prevent sounds made by you being accidentally interpreted as paranormal noises. For example, you walk in and check the tapes and cough, but you don't remember doing it and didn't announce yourself. You listen back to the tape and lo and behold an EVP that sounds like a cough is present – because you don't remember making the noise, you identify it as paranormal. Obviously, if a camera is filming at the same time, this isn't a problem.

Ouija board

And now we come to the most infamous of all experiments into the paranormal – the legendary ouija board. The word 'ouija' is a combination of two words for yes – the French word 'oui' and the German word 'ja'.

The ouija board is a simple communication device, it is a board with the alphabet, numbers and the words 'yes' and 'no'

BELOW Never leave home without a video camera with Night Shot. Video footage is crucial as it can help to capture the atmosphere, as well as light anomalies and EVP. Locking–off video cameras allows you to investigate elsewhere, without missing any possible activity.

written upon it. A wine glass or something similar is usually placed upon the board, the participants place a finger upon it and the glass moves towards individual letters to spell words or answer yes/no questions. The glass used is believed to be moved by a spirit tapping into the energy of the people touching the glass.

Here is the procedure for using an ouija board:

1. Place the board on a level, stable surface, such as a table.

2. Place an upturned glass on the board.

3. Set up an overhead video recorder to record the whole board. When your team is happy with the set up you can switch on the camera. If other cameras are available, they should be set up to record the rest of the site in which the experiment is taking place.

4. Set up a dictaphone or a tape recorder and start to make a sound recording. These devices should be placed both close to the team and around the room.

5. Take baseline readings for the site, including temperature and humidity. You may want to take several readings as the

experiment proceeds to see whether these measurements change significantly.

6. Selected members of the team should now place a single finger on the base of the upturned glass. One person should assume responsibility for asking the questions. This individual should ask any spirits present to communicate with you by moving the glass.

7. When the glass starts to move, ask relevant questions for the spirit to answer, such as their name.

8. A member of the team should note down the responses from the glass as it moves. Alternatively, you can speak them out loud and record them.

9. When the glass no longer moves or the team decides to end the experiment, take a final set of baselines.

10. Stop all recording devices.

11. Listen to and watch the tapes, noting down anything unusual in the normal manner. Archive the media and any notes made during the experiment.

Much controversy surrounds the use of ouija boards. There is scepticism as to their reliability, and most cases of the planchette or glass moving can be attributed to 'idiomotive response' or a fraudulent participant. Trying to eliminate these factors can be tricky. Idiomotive movement is a naturally occurring response to a situation that is unknowingly performed by a participant. If you suspect anyone of fraudulent practices, ask them politely to leave the experiment. Not everyone approves of using ouija boards to communicate with spirits and their opinion should be respected. If members of your team do not want to participate you should not force them to do so.

BELOW *The ouija or spirit board is said to be a method of communication with the spirit world. Spirits, using your energy, can move the planchette and talk by spelling out words and sentences.*

TRIGGER OBJECTS

A trigger object is an item that is used to elicit a response from an alleged spirit. The idea is that the spirit spots the object and investigates it or moves it. Meanwhile, you record the interaction between the spirit and the trigger object. These experiments are easy to set up, record and replicate.

There are no specific rules as to what these objects should be, but a degree of common sense should be applied. For example, don't use objects that are likely to cause immediate harm to people or property, such as fireworks or firearms and other weaponry.

Trigger objects should be relevant to the investigation or relate to the culture of the alleged spirit being investigated (see pages 33–36). For example, you could place a Catholic artefact in an abandoned building of that faith or a coin dating to a relevant year if a specific reference is known — if the spirit is alleged to be a remnant of the civil war, then a coin from that period may work.

Size is another consideration — most trigger objects should be portable, as it means that there is a good chance they can be moved with little effort by any spirits present. Larger objects can be also be used as necessary, as they may provoke some interesting activity from alleged spirits coming to observe them. For example, placing an old car at an area thought to be haunted by the victim of a road accident or a phantom hitchhiker could yield positive results.

The Haunted Britain team uses the following procedures to conduct small trigger object experiments:

1. Carefully select your trigger object or objects.

2. Conduct baseline tests — take standard EMF, humidity and temperature measurements for the area, and the trigger objects.

ABOVE *Roman armour brooches used as a trigger object for the haunting of a Centurion Soldier.*

3. Ensure the surface area that you are using is level. Take a piece of paper and arrange the objects upon it. If possible, use a piece of graph paper and place a set of small archaeological camera scales alongside the items. This will give you an accurate scale when you are filming or photographing the objects — it also provides you with a reference point, so that you can see how far an object may have moved.

4. Carefully trace around the objects so that an outline remains on the paper when they are removed. Reset the objects and scales if they moved while you were tracing around them.

5. Now take a photograph of the set up from a direct overhead position. This will be your reference point so that you can assess any movement. Make sure that you have all the objects and the scale in the photograph. You can also take a

photograph of the objects from the front if this is relevant; for example, if you are using a toy bear to bring forth a child spirit, and you initially position the bear so that it has its face pointing into the room, you need to take a photograph of the object in this position in case it moves to face another direction when you leave the area. Using just the overhead photograph for reference may not help you to assess whether anything has happened.

6. If required, set up the motion detectors, preferably of the type that use beams to detect movement. If using something like the toy bear, the beam should be placed in front of the object. If the item is flat, for example, a coin, the beam should be placed above it.

7. Now set a camcorder up, preferably using a tripod, which can easily film any or all of the trigger object(s). If possible set up other cameras around the room to film the trigger objects from several different angles.

8. Leave the area in which you have placed the trigger objects and, if possible, investigate elsewhere at the site. If the motion detectors signal movement you have two choices: you can either return to the objects to see why the alarms have gone off and reset the beam alarm, or you can leave the area alone and allow the detectors to reset themselves. The latter option is preferable, as the other cameras will still be recording the rest of the room and the trigger objects. That said, checking the site instantly may give you the opportunity to catch a paranormal incident as it actually happens.

9. Once you return to the trigger objects take photographs, as you did in step five. Note whether the objects have moved. It is important to remember NOT to touch the trigger objects at this point.

BELOW *After locking the room and leaving a camera trained on the brooch, we can see it has moved during the investigation. By using contextual trigger objects the Haunted Britain team garner more results.*

TOP TEN MISTAKES

1. BEING RUDE
Not thanking the venue owner or manager is a bad thing to do and could impact on both your investigation and subsequent investigations. Always remember to thank everybody involved.

2. NOT APPLYING A CULTURAL CONTEXT TO THE POSSIBILITY OF A GHOST
When researching the spirit activity at a location, make thorough notes of the time period in which they were alive. This will allow you better communication with the spirit.

For example, speaking to a Roman soldier in English could yield positive results, but speaking to them in Latin may yield even better ones.

3. NOT DOING RESEARCH
It is strongly recommended that you conduct research into the location, as you may uncover more than you bargained for. This ties directly into point two.

4. ASSUMING EVERYTHING IS PARANORMAL
Only when no other explanation for phenomena can be given, can evidence be put forward of paranormal activity.

5. JUST WATCHING THE VIDEO FOOTAGE, BUT NOT LISTENING
It is highly recommended that you watch each video of your paranormal investigation a number of times, as you may pick up more the second, third or even fourth time you watch it.

Pay close attention to the sound in your video, and try to ignore any background noise. Make sure you are aware of any noises that could be explained away.

6. HAVING TEAMS MADE UP OF A SINGLE SEX
By having an all male, or all female team, you could miss out on the opportunity to capture phenomena at work.

7. TAKING EVERYTHING TOO SERIOUSLY!
Investigating the paranormal can be an arduous and often unrewarding affair. You can quickly become unfocused and miss evidence. By taking breaks and relaxing with your team-mates you will allow yourself to calm down and approach different areas of your location with a refreshed attitude.

8. REUSING CASSETTES
Never reuse audio or video cassettes if you have used them during your investigation. This may make the prospect of investigating the paranormal more expensive, but by doing this, you eliminate the chances of evidence being just the result of sounds or images existing on re-used tape.

We recommend using DVD camcorders, or those that record direct to flash cards. These can wiped and formatted, and you eliminate any possibility of the above.

9. NOT LISTENING TO SUGGESTIONS OF YOUR TEAM MEMBERS AND PROPRIETORS
Just because you cannot explain the phenomena you are catching, doesn't mean somebody else cannot. Be open to other points of view from your group and also those of the venue's owners – after all they know the location better than anybody.

10. GOING TO LOCATIONS ALONE
Never, never, never attend an investigation alone. It has been known for people to lie in wait for paranormal investigators, as you will invariably be carrying a lot of expensive equipment that can easily be sold.

Let people know where you will be, and keep a mobile phone with you at all times – nothing is worth more than your personal safety.

WITNESS RECORD SHEET

Location

Type of phenomenon. Please tick corresponding box.

| Apparition | ☐ | Possession | ☐ | Noise | ☐ | Light anomaly | ☐ |
| Voice | ☐ | Feeling | ☐ | Touch | ☐ | Poltergeist | ☐ |

Other. Please specify

Date and time

No. of witnesses

Where did you see or feel this phenomena?

Did you know of any haunting?

How did the location feel prior to the experience?

How did the location feel after the experience?

Please describe exactly what you experienced

Declaration   Name: Signed: Date:

BASELINE RECORD SHEET

Location

Area investigated	Temp °C	Lux	Humidity	Noise	M/Waves

Equipment used

Notes on location - i.e. draughts, noises etc.

Declaration   Name: Signed: Date:

1.   **Environment Meter.** This piece of equipment is almost as essential as the EMF Meter, with variable settings for light, noise, temperature and humidity. The Environment Meter is best used as a constant measuring device of the ambient room conditions. This allows you to gauge, quickly and accurately, any fluctuations that may occur.

2.   **Dictaphone.** Again, another essential piece of equipment, commonly used to try and catch EVP (Electronic Voice Phenomena) or ASP (Anomalous Sound Phenomena). From experience, you should never go any-where without one running as EVP / ASP can occur when you least expect it. The Haunted Britain team uses dicta-phones in two ways. They can be left in a locked-off room to record any phenomena that happens while no-one is there. This allows evidence to be collected without interference from outside sources. The other way is to have the dictaphone recording during vigils to capture any

anomalous noises that occur whilst carrying out the investigation. It is important in these circumstances to have everyone in the room speaking clearly (not whispering) so that any underlying voices can be distinguished.

3.   **Thermometers.** Cold spots are a noted part of paranormal investigations, and all ghost hunters should be equipped with a thermometer (either digital or a common household one). This will enable you to easily quan-tify any reports of cold spots or strange phenomena that may occur during your investigation.

4.   **Torches or Glow Sticks.** These are the most important part of any ghost hunter's kit, as being safe on an investigation is of primary concern to all. Each member of the Haunted Britain team has a torch at their disposal. They can also be used to quickly identify where phenomena are occuring ... but above all, never go on a paranormal investi-gation without one!

5.   **Motion Detectors.** These are not essential pieces of equipment, however the results gained from them can be amazing. Motion Detectors are used to lock off rooms where paranormal activity has been reported. A small laser beam is projected from one detector to another, and if the beam is broken an alarm is sounded. They are best used when reports of wandering spirits are prevalant.

6.   **EMF Meter.** Again, another essential piece of equipment for the ghost hunter's kit. An EMF Meter will allow you to quickly establish any unusual fluctuations in electrical fields, you can also quickly discount any strange readings by running them along the walls during your baseline investigations to establish sources of power (plug sockets etc).

7.   **Camcorder.** The camcorder is another piece of equipment that comes highly recommended. You may see something outstanding, and therefore a camcorder could capture what the world has been waiting for. The Haunted Britain team recommend camcorders with Night Shot and Super Night Shot, also ones that do not need a light to function in the dark.

8.   **Trigger Objects.** These are relevant items left for any spirits to interact with. The Haunted Britain team leave items which apply to the era in which the spirit was alive. It is important to note that you have to apply a cultural context to your trigger objects, using Victorian coins with the ghost of a Roman soldier will usually not garner results. For example, using Victorian dolls in an old Victorian work-house where children were employed, would make more sense.

INVESTIGATIONS

Haunted Britain are often contacted to conduct investigations at various locations around the UK. It is important to note that when entering and planning an investigation, you must enter with an open mind that ghosts and the paranormal may or may not exist.

Our objective on an investigation is to try and quantify what previous witnesses have reported and seen, by trying to capture the reported phenomena using various types of scientific equipment and of course the five senses. However, on most investigations it seems that the team can start out investigating one subject and finish trying to explain something completely different that has occurred during the night.

For example, on an investigation at the Talbot Hotel in Northamptonshire, we initially began to investigate the numerous reports of Mary, Queen of Scots being seen on the staircase. However, what we came away with was a rather eerie EVP speaking directly to a member of the team… and it is with this in mind that you must remain open-minded before, during and after your investigation.

Haunted Britain always stand by the phrase:
'Only after no other explanation can be found, could it possibly be counted as paranormal?'

THE WORSHIPFUL COMPANY OF BARBERS SURGEONS
BARBERS SURGEONS' HALL, CITY OF LONDON

PREVIOUS SIGHTINGS AND EXPERIENCES

• Soldiers in the basement – possibly Roman in origin
• Orbs in various areas of the building
• Presences felt in the Great Hall, Court Room and basement
• A young woman walking around the perimeter of the hall
• Cold spots and areas of intense pressure
• Feelings of oppression
• Strange occurrences within the Hans Holbein painting, which hangs in the Great Hall, including colours and facial expressions changing

THE LOCATION

Nestled in the heart of the City of London, a stone's throw from the Museum of London and the Barbican, stands Barbers Surgeons' Hall. It has occupied the same area since the 1440s, although the appearance of the hall has altered dramatically since it was first built, as it was damaged in the Second World War and rebuilt in 1969.

The first hall was much smaller and functioned as offices until 1607 when a Court Room was added. After some restoration, an anatomical theatre was built in 1635 where lectures and

ABOVE The admittance of a member into the prestigious Barbers Surgeons Guild. OPPOSITE The lavish Coat of Arms of the Worshipful Company of Barbers Surgeons.

demonstrations were held. At about the same time, a new Great Parlour was introduced for formal functions and gatherings. Unfortunately, the Great Fire of London in 1666 destroyed many buildings in the area, including much of Barbers Surgeons' Hall, leaving only the anatomy theatre intact.

After reconstruction, Barbers Surgeons' Hall remained substantially the same, until 1784 when the anatomy theatre was demolished to make way for housing. It was never rebuilt, primarily because the Royal College of Surgeons built their own premises for this purpose some years later.

The building became one of many casualties of the destructive air raids carried out during the Blitz in 1940, and it was all but demolished. Luckily, however, like many people with substantial wealth and historical objects, the Barbers Surgeons had moved their possessions and valuable artefacts to a secure location when war broke out in 1939.

The building you can see today was opened in May 1969 by Queen Elizabeth, the Queen Mother, who revisited the hall in 2000 to reveal the new Millennium Window that was dedicated to her. The new building is much larger than its predecessors, and incorporates cellars and offices in addition to the Great Hall, Court Room, library, Charter Room, reception room and quarters for the Master. The artefacts preserved during the many periods of demolition are now on prominent display, some dating back to the 14th century.

The surroundings are initially a little peculiar. The London Wall runs parallel to the building and part of it is integrated into the gardens. The area in which the hall is situated was once part of a large Roman fort, plans of which can be seen at the Museum of London.

Given the area's history, and the obvious link to Roman London, it seems strange and in some ways disappointing that the brightly illuminated, high-rise office buildings of the modern city dominate the landscape. Barbers Surgeons' Hall stands in stark contrast to its surroundings, exuding history and heritage and intriguing many a passer-by.

THE HISTORY

The organization of Barbers Surgeons is one of London's oldest established guilds and is ranked 17th in the livery companies' order of precedence. The guild came into being in 1308, when Richard the Barber was elected to keep order within the trade. The Lord Mayor and aldermen of the City gave him the right 'to make a diligent search through the whole of his craft every month, and if he shall find any brothel keeper or other disreputable folk to the scandal of the craft, he shall detain them and cause them to be brought before the chamber'. The company also included a number of surgeons, the first of whom was recorded in 1312.

Unlike their modern counterparts, who mainly stick to cutting hair and shaving, the barbers of previous centuries also performed surgical and medical tasks, including dentistry. Many medical ailments were treated using a practice known as 'bleeding', as it was believed that most conditions originated from 'bad blood' in the system.

The amalgamation of the Surgeons' Guild, and the Company of Barbers took place in 1540 through an Act of Parliament. One of the privileges granted to the new company was the annual allocation of four bodies for dissection. These unfortunate individuals were passed on to the guild from Tyburn, London's notorious gallows. This was a major step forward for the guild, as they were now permitted to practise dissection for scientific purposes. It helped to pave the way for modern surgical procedures and the understanding of the human body, matters that we take for granted today.

The guild boasted the largest number of freemen of any the City's livery companies. The two disciplines were always kept separate and neither trade was permitted to perform the work of the other. The association between barbers and surgeons continued for many years, although it was rarely a peaceful relationship, as there were many disputes that needed to be resolved.

By the 18th century, the strains caused by the alliance between barbers and surgeons had started to take their toll on the guild. The work taken on by surgeons required greater skills as time progressed and their numbers were growing, due in part to the prestige that the title brought with it. Eventually, the surgeons petitioned the House of Commons, asking for the two professions to be formally separated, and royal assent was granted in May 1745. The barbers retained the hall, along with certain treasures relating to the guild's history. The Surgeons' Guild relocated to their own premises until 1800, when the Royal College of Surgeons was founded.

Today the Worshipful Company of Barbers Surgeons has a limited connection with the trade from which it takes its name, but it still maintains strong links with medicine, particularly surgery, as many of the company's members are associated with the profession.

REMOTE VIEWING EXPERIMENT

A week before the investigation into Barbers Surgeons' Hall began, a floor plan of the location was placed on the Haunted Britain website as part of a remote viewing experiment. The layout of the building was posted, along with the outlines and name of each room. No other information about the hall and its surroundings were given. Visitors to the site were then asked to email the team stating the area on the plan that they thought played host to the most paranormal activity.

Remote viewing is a known psychic phenomenon that has been the subject of much exploration since the early 20th century, particularly by the American and British intelligence agencies. Plans or maps of a location are given to the participants. All that is required of them is that they clear their minds and concentrate on the plans. They then choose a location that they feel is the most active in paranormal terms.

Some believe that the results of these experiments are the result of extra-sensory perception (ESP), but the experiment in its truest form doesn't require any particular psychic ability. There are many explanations and theories as to how a final choice is made. Some are made scientifically, some are attributed to the paranormal, and others merely choose a site that sparks interest. For the experiment on Barbers Surgeons' Hall the Haunted Britain team were not concerned by how locations were chosen. The purpose of the remote investigation was to explore whether there was any truth to claims that paranormal activity can be sensed from a 2-D image. With very little historical information available on the hall and paranormal activity witnessed here, this was the ideal opportunity to test such a theory.

Strangely, the remote experiment presented a clear frontrunner, as over 70 per cent of the participants selected the same location. Most of the individuals who contacted the site said that they felt drawn to the Great Hall. Another 20 per cent chose the Court Room, and five per cent felt that the reception hall was the most active area. Other areas included were the basement and Charter Room. But were the sites chosen during the remote viewing experiment actually the most active paranormal areas? It remained to be seen.

BELOW *The enormous Holbein painting of King Henry VIII. It is said that the people within this painting move, and can also follow you around the room.*

THE INVESTIGATION BEGINS

Haunted Britain was the first group to do an extensive paranormal investigation into Barbers Surgeons' Hall, so there was no previous research on the subject to feed the team's imaginations. All they knew was that the building's occupants had experienced things that they couldn't explain.

The interview with the Beadle of the Barbers Surgeons' Company proved interesting, but he was careful not to reveal anything that could cloud the team's judgement or allow any preconceptions to distort the investigation. This particular member of the company had lived at the site for many years and was aware of many paranormal presences in the building. Some were described as friendly, others not so genial — that was all he told the team.

Walking to Barbers Surgeons' Hall, the team passed the old London Wall and walked through the grounds of the ruined St Olave's Church. This was where the corpses of the dissected criminals from Tyburn were taken for burial. A nice thought to contend with while strolling through the area in the dark!

Accompanied by the Beadle, the Haunted Britain team entered the gardens that encircled the hall. The part of London Wall that still stands in the grounds was clearly visible as they approached the building. Two members of the team had already begun to feel uneasy about the surroundings and felt like they were being watched — neither of them wanted to venture any closer to the ancient wall than necessary.

The Beadle then explained that the area behind the wall, which now houses the herb garden, was an old burial pit that was used to dispose of plague victims. Taking the team around the wall he pointed out a small mound and a stone placed beneath a withered tree. An unmarked grave lay there — an eerie place if ever there was one.

As the team walked around the outside of the building, the last member in the group felt a sharp tug on the back of his jacket. He stopped and looked behind him, but there was nobody there. Looking around for a logical explanation for what had happened, such as overhanging branches, fencing or protrusions on the walls that could have snagged the jacket, the team could not find any notable cause for what he had felt. Had they already caught the attention of one of the ghosts of the Barbers Surgeons?

INSIDE THE HALL

Entering through the back of the building, the team were taken on a tour of the public areas used by the company. The main reception area is highly decorated, with wooden panels and imposing pictures of past masters of the guild staring

ABOVE *The beautiful Millennium stained-glass window dedicated by HRH Queen Elizabeth, The Queen Mother, in 2000.*

down on the patrons below. The stained glass of the Millennium Window shines down over the stairwell. Surrounding this are a number of wooden panels engraved with the names and dates of past Masters of the guild, dating back to 1376.

Leading the team around the building, the Beadle explained how the Worshipful Company of Barbers Surgeons operates today and explained elements of its history. He was still very careful not to mention anything about the paranormal experiences that he and other individuals had encountered in the building. Nevertheless, it was clear that he had an aversion to the basement. He was wary of going into the room alone, even though he used it every day he was not happy to do so, particularly for the purposes of a paranormal investigation.

The team gathered in the reception hall to devise a plan of action. It was agreed that there were definite areas and rooms that seemed to exude a particular feeling. The Great Hall had been selected as the most atmospheric room by the visitors to the website and it certainly appeared that something in it gave everyone the sense that they were not going to be disappointed by their investigations. The Court Room also felt somewhat unnerving, particularly for one

ABOVE *The Main Hall of the Barbers Surgeons. In a room this size it is good to keep all team members present and have equipment located in different areas.*

member of the team. During the team's initial tour of the building, she had felt a tap on the top of her head when walking through that room. She was the last one to exit the room, so no other member of the party could have done this to her.

And then there was the basement – the Beadle's apprehension of this room was enough to intrigue the team, and, if his reluctance was anything to go by, we thought the presence here might not be of a friendly nature.

THE GREAT HALL

With the lights on, the Great Hall is welcoming, warm and opulent. With the lights off and curtains drawn it seems overpowering, intense and almost sinister. The focal point of this large room is the imposing painting by Hans Holbein, which shows Henry VIII signing the 1540 treaty that amalgamated the barbers and surgeons. The scene depicts the charter being handed to Thomas Vicary, who was the king's Serjeant-Surgeon at the time and Master of the Company.

Evidence found in the wreckage of Henry's great warship, the *Mary Rose*, suggested that one of the doomed crewmembers was a surgeon and member of the company. A black surgeon's cap and instruments were retrieved when the wreckage was raised from the bottom of the sea in 1982. The artefacts were returned to the guild and are on display in the Great Hall. Could the owner of these possessions be returning to his place of work?

The Beadle then brought out a chalice that belonged to the 17th-century monarch, Charles II. The vessel is adorned with acorns, which hang around the bowl and would have been jingled to signify to servants that it was empty and in need of filling. One of the team picked up the chalice and waved it in front of the painting of Henry VIII and we asked him to come and use his prized possession. Unfortunately, Henry didn't seem react – at least not to the naked eye – but two singular, large orbs were caught on successive photographs taken at the scene.

Two team members stood in the domed window, which was where 70 per cent of those involved in the remote viewing experiment felt that the activity would be high. The pair felt a sudden urge to look through the curtains and out of the window – they immediately noticed something unusual – something that could explain why so many people had been drawn to this particular spot.

Directly outside the window was the site of the old plague pit, the grave and the place where a team member had felt his jacket being tugged. This was rendered even stranger by the fact that that the plans shown on the website were just floor plans – they included no indication of the exact location of the hall or its surroundings. Even the team had no idea about the proximity or existence of the burial sites, prior to their tour of the building. The situation intrigued everybody — could this be the paranormal energy that the remote participants had somehow tuned into?

With so much reported activity and plenty of locations to investigate, the team decided to split up. One group stayed in the Great Hall, while two members investigated the Court Room.

SOMEONE WANTS TO MAKE CONTACT...

The team in the Great Hall placed themselves at different spots around the room. Baseline tests on the walk around the area had revealed no significant readings on the EMF Meters or draughts from external sources. The team carried on with their attempts to communicate with any spirits. After a few minutes, something drew one of the team into the far corner of the room, just to the right of the Holbein painting. The EMF Meter suddenly started to screech, its reading was around 6 milligauss (the unit that measures the strength of a magnetic field) — a great deal higher than the signal emitted by plug sockets and standard light fittings, all of which had been turned off. The reading seemed to get stronger towards the corner of the room and along one side of the wall.

Then the EMF Meter stopped abruptly and showed no reading at all. The investigator pushed a button to reactivate the device, but nothing happened. If the reading stemmed from an electrical source, it would remain constant. It stayed as it was for a few more minutes, and then, as though someone had just flicked a switch, it began screeching again at between 7–8 milligauss. Suddenly, the temperature dropped, it was as if someone had opened a door — but there were no doors anywhere nearby.

The investigator took a seat in the area that seemed most affected. The EMF Meter still showed high readings, and activity seemed to be focusing around her. There was nothing on her person that could cause the readings, as the entire team had emptied their pockets, and it couldn't be explained why the measurements weren't constant. She stretched her arm out and the meter stopped; she brought it back into her body and the meter started up again. She repeated the process using both arms separately — the meter stopped when it was away from her body but screeched when it was brought back towards it.

This activity lasted for about another 20 seconds. Then, just as before, the screeching suddenly stopped. The reset button was pushed,

but once again nothing happened. Suddenly, she felt a blast of cold air in her face and the EMF Meter went off the scale. Feeling extremely uncomfortable, the researcher jumped out of the chair and moved closer to the rest of the team.

'HE'S FOLLOWED ME, HASN'T HE?'

The other team members were seated on the other side of the room, from where they had witnessed the unusual activity. At first, everything seemed to calm down, but within a couple of minutes the chilling air returned and the team member who had experienced the phenomenon said 'He's back isn't he? ... he's followed me hasn't he?'

Another member of the team picked up on the spirit that appeared to have followed her colleague across the room. As a sensitive, she had a strong feeling that his name was James or Jamie. He was only young, probably about 15 years old, and he had been sentenced to death for theft, but protested his innocence. The team started to ask him questions, and more answers appeared to come through. A date in the early 16th century was given — James seemed very angry that his body had been dissected and that he had not been given a proper burial.

BELOW *One of the Haunted Britain members, Carolyn, later described seeing a white ball of light right in front of her. Little did we realize we had caught it on camera.*

ABOVE *A strange face is captured by digital camera, when the only people present were taking the photograph or behind the camera.*

The atmosphere and mood in the room changed. Immense sorrow and sadness came over the team, and it became far too much for the two members who had made contact with the young spirit. They couldn't describe what was happening, but it felt as if this boy was lonely and searching for something. Perhaps it was a relative, an explanation of what had happened to him or simply justice – they could not be sure. Unfortunately, it was something that they would not be able to help him find.

Strangely, a picture taken shortly after this experience showed a clear and bright light anomaly in front of the team around the spot where they had all felt the spirit had stood. It appears that the team member who had made contact with the young boy was looking directly at the light.

MEANWHILE...

In the Court Room, more activity was being witnessed. The team members who had elected to hold vigils here felt drawn to it. A great deal smaller than the Great Hall, the Court Room has a very formal and almost pompous ambience and everything about it feels judicial and important. The Master's

desk is placed proudly along the back wall, along with his large, imposing chair and gavel. The walls are decorated with yet more portraits of past Masters, who look down on people present in the court.

Earlier in the evening, as the team went around the building to set up their equipment, two female team-members entered the Court Room to close the curtains. Until recently, this would have been somewhat unusual, as the Company of Barbers Surgeons has only recently admitted their first female member, so it is a rarity for a woman to be present in this room, especially with no link to the organization or one of its members. As the two women left the room they decided to take a photograph in the direction of the door.

Looking at the screen of the digital camera, they noticed a strange white shape in the glass window. When the image was enlarged a bearded man wearing a black cap appeared to be looking through the glass. What was even more unusual was that the light in the corridor had cast a shadow of the man onto the wooden panels. Every portrait, mirror and panel in the immediate vicinity was checked and it was confirmed that the image could not be recreated or attributed to anything natural. Could someone have been keeping an eye on the two women in the Court Room?

Extremely black, cold and daunting, the Court Room took on an even more ominous aura. A feeling of oppression and belligerence hung in the air. A series of bangs and taps seemed to respond to the requests of the team members and it was felt that whoever was present really didn't appreciate the women being there. Despite further questioning, no further contact seemed to have been made at this time – but both agreed that the room deserved further investigation later.

'YOU'RE NOT GETTING ME DOWN THERE!'

Taking the proverbial 'bull by the horns', the team ventured down to the basement. Seeming rather reticent about this decision, the Beadle initially held back. A little gentle persuasion from the rest of the team convinced him to join the excursion. It appeared that the prospect of staying upstairs alone was more daunting.

His reaction begged the question of what it was that lurked down there that made him so wary. But also, what was upstairs that he dared not be left alone with? Even though he lives with this presence on a daily basis, the Beadle admitted to the team that he tries not to be on his own at night. Whatever he had seen, heard or experienced in the hall had obviously had a lasting affect.

Unusually for a basement, the room seemed relatively calm, light and airy. The air temperature was naturally much cooler than upstairs. With the lights on, it was quite inviting. Then the lights went out. It was tense for a few moments, but once their eyes had adjusted to the darkness, the team agreed that it wasn't as scary as they were expecting.

Aware that a basement houses a lot of dust, the team tried to keep their movements to a minimum. A static video camera was set up in the far right-hand corner of the room, and the group remained to the other side of the room as much as possible.

Three digital cameras were used at different points around the room, so that anything significant would be caught on at least one device. Initially, the images all contained a snowstorm effect that was caused by dust, eventually this settled and the pictures became clearer.

After ten minutes, it was noticed that each camera was picking up the same two or three light anomalies in the centre of the room. What was more unusual was that these orbs changed colour — some were blue, some orange and some white, but they always appeared to stay in one area.

BELOW Two of the Haunted Britain team members begin to feel the presence of a young boy named James.

For the same orbs to appear in a similar position on three cameras was very bizarre, and something that the team could not find any practical and natural reason for. It was even stranger that the same orbs were also caught on the video camera.

One team member sensed that the group was being watched, particularly from the main door into the room. Unfortunately, because the trigger for the automatic lighting was near the door, the investigators couldn't take any EMF or temperature readings. However, if the light came on without anybody standing near the sensor, it would go some way to confirm her suspicions. Two separate photographs revealed a large orb to one side of the door. Again, these could not be attributed to natural causes, such as reflections or other light sources. Had someone or something followed them?

After another 15 minutes with no activity the team started to feel a little disappointed. Then, the sensitive within the team started to feel the presence of a young girl. She tried to communicate with her, and eventually she received the name 'Mary'. Further questioning revealed that this spirit was looking for her brother — could this be James from the Great Hall?

Information seemed to be coming thick and fast. Mary's brother had been taken from her family at an early age and

BELOW *Various apparitions have been seen in the basement area of the Barbers Surgeons' Guild Hall, and two team members sensed a presence at the entrance.*

BEING NICE GETS RESULTS

Drained after their experience in the basement, the team took a quick break and discussed where they needed to conduct a final investigation. The Court Room was a must, and so the men in the team decided to take a camera and an EMF Meter with them to see if the individual captured during the previous visit would return.

The rest of the team split themselves between the reception room and the Great Hall. Something was playing on their minds. If James and Mary were present in the basement and had, as it seemed, passed on together, would the EMF Meter readings still be high in the area where James was first encountered? Armed with two EMF Meters, a team member set off to check.

A definite change in atmosphere and mood greeted her — the room felt much warmer and more comfortable. Moving into the area where she had recorded the high EMF readings, she activated the meter again. Unbelievably, there was no reading at all. Puzzled and very intrigued, she used another EMF Meter, but that showed the same result — there was no fluctuation. Had the spirit of James passed to his rightful resting place? All the findings suggested that this was a distinct possibility.

The team in the Great Hall carried out further vigils, but apart from a few more orbs, which were caught on both digital and video camera, nothing else unusual was detected. Meanwhile, activity was picking up in the Court Room. The two members of the team who had elected to re-investigate the site had started to yield even more positive results.

An EMF Meter was placed on the Judge's desk. Questions were asked and it was requested that the spirit made the EMF Meter click if the answer was 'yes'. The investigators began by being forceful, but this tactic didn't seem to work and nothing happened. It was deduced that maybe this spirit required a certain degree of manners and decorum.

The change in tone immediately generated a reaction, and the meter started to produce clicks in response to the

brought to Barbers Surgeons' Hall after his death. She had also died young, since then she had been searching around the building and waiting for her sibling. All the information seemed to point to the young boy that the team had encountered earlier. Forming a circle, the team started a séance to help these trapped souls cross over and be reunited.

Just after the circle had been formed, video footage captured two large orbs moving towards the group. A quiet female voice was also heard in the corner of the room away from the circle.

The group concentrated on passing their energy around the circle. The energy intensified extremely quickly. One member of the circle started to fall backwards and those either side had to fight to keep him on his feet. With this energy building, the Beadle's legs started to buckle. Everyone felt the pressure accumulating, and many present described a sensation that felt as if their stomach and chest were being pulled into the circle. Within minutes, the atmosphere in the room became electric. Then the energy dropped rapidly. The feelings and sensations experienced by the group dissipated. Had these poor souls crossed over? The team would probably never know for sure.

ABOVE *The chalice of King Henry VIII was used as a form of trigger object. The chalice is far too highly-prized to move, so an EMF Meter was placed close by.*

SUMMARY OF THE INVESTIGATION

The investigation into Barber Surgeons' Hall had definitely provided Haunted Britain with some interesting results. Without a doubt, the hall is visited by the spirits of those who used to frequent the building or were associated with the practices that took place there. Some are grounded, such as James, who felt trapped, while others are like the lady in the Court Room, who revisits the hall whenever she pleases.

Whether or not you believe in séances and helping spirits to pass over, the activity in one room was so intense that it cannot be dismissed, particularly as it disappeared once the séance had taken place. However, it would be interesting to find out if anything occurred there again after the team had gone.

By far the most significant evidence collected from this location was the photograph of the man standing in the window of the Court Room door. After much scrutiny and analysis by experts, the image was found to be genuine and it could not be recreated.

However, despite all the positive results gathered at Barber Surgeons' Hall, it was felt that more activity was waiting to be uncovered than had been revealed during this investigation, particularly in the basement. It is definitely one location that the team would like to investigate again.

team's enquiries. Further questions were asked at random intervals to make sure this was not a natural occurrence and some questions were repeated to test if they got the same answers. It genuinely appeared that someone was trying to communicate.

From the responses it appeared that this person was a woman. She was not someone who worked in the building, but a wife of one of the previous Masters of the Worshipful Company of Barbers Surgeons. By meticulously calling out centuries, decades and years, the team managed to elicit a date from the spirit. With the information gained, the team pursued further research and came up with a name for this lady's husband, he was not particularly prominent in the company, but it appeared that his wife was more attached to the building than he was.

Excited by the activity the men asked the whole team to join them. Instantly, the sounds ceased. Nothing happened, but many of the group felt that they were being watched. Was this woman just shy? Shortly afterwards, one of the video cameras turned itself off for no apparent reason. There was plenty of battery power and the tape had plenty of recording time left. Was this the result of paranormal interference?

The team agreed that the equipment was upsetting the spirit, so they turned off all the cameras. There was still no reaction. Eventually it was decided that the rest of the group should depart, with just the men remaining. No sooner had this happened, than the clicks returned. Communication carried on for a further ten minutes then the responses stopped. Somewhat disappointed that their exploits hadn't been caught on tape, the men decided to wrap up their investigation. Neither of them had any doubt that someone had made contact with them and they felt delighted that she appeared to respond to their questions. Unfortunately, whoever it was had left the room.

THE WORSHIPFUL COMPANY OF SADDLERS
SADDLERS' HALL, CITY OF LONDON

PREVIOUS SIGHTINGS AND EXPERIENCES

• Loud bangs that sound like doors slamming shut
• The appearance of a decomposing woman in the Tunnel Room
• Pounding knocks on various doors, particularly the Beadle's flat
• Footsteps in various rooms and along corridors
• Rattling cutlery and clinking of glasses in the Great Hall
• The sounds of parties in full swing in the Great Hall
• The image of a ghostly person appearing on a publicity photo taken in the Great Hall
• The sound of Second World War bombers flying overhead
• Keys jangling in the clerk's office
• The smell of death and decay between the lift and silver safe in the basement
• Cold spots and feelings of oppression in various areas
• Two apparitions in the basement that are thought to be a vicar and his wife, whose ashes were kept at the hall

THE LOCATION

Just a few yards from St Paul's Cathedral, off an ancient byway, is the magnificent Mansion House of the Worshipful Company of Saddlers. The building on view today is the fourth incarnation of Saddlers' Hall, which has occupied the same site for the last 600 years. The land was originally a medieval freehold and larger in area than the modern plot.

It is thought that the first hall was completed in 1395 to coincide with the Incorporation Charter, and references to Saddlers' Hall appear in documents from the early 1400s. It occupied an area of land on Westchepe, originally known as 'The Saddlery'. The building was commissioned by William de Lincolne, who was elected to safeguard the ordinances of the Saddlers' Guild. De Lincolne bequeathed 10 marks in his will, which were to be put towards the construction of a permanent residence that the Saddlers could use as a place for meetings and gatherings.

The first building was destroyed in the Great Fire of London in 1666. In 1670 a replacement was built at great expense, although many of the original artefacts and documents had perished. In 1821 the second Saddlers' Hall was destroyed by another fire, and the building was declared beyond reasonable restoration.

The third hall lasted until 1940, when the bombing raids of the Blitz destroyed much of the surrounding area. Extensive re-planning of the City of London reduced the size of the original freehold. Losing its former frontage on Cheapside, the new Saddlers' Hall was built on a smaller portion of the land that had been awarded to the Company in the 12th century.

Today, the surrounding area is dominated by high-rise office buildings, which swamp many of the historical establishments that have occupied the area for centuries. The City of London still contains a large number of Livery Halls, including the Guildhall of London, Pewterers' Hall, Barbers Surgeons' Hall (see pages 56–65), Goldsmiths' Hall, Plaisterers' Hall and the Wax-Chandlers' Hall, to name but a few. Unfortunately, the architecture of the modern world has painted these premises into the background, but if you venture into the midst of Cheapside and look around,

there may be more history than first realized nestling in London's back streets.

THE HISTORY

It is thought that the history of the Saddlers' Company goes as far back as the Anglo-Saxon period, before the Norman Conquest of 1066. However, few documents exist to verify the exact date that the Guild was formed, as many of its official papers were damaged by the fires that ravaged the buildings. However, it is believed that the Worshipful Company of Saddlers is one of the oldest of London's Livery Companies with evidence of the trade dating back to 1179.

The Saddlers' first Royal Charter was awarded by Edward I in 1272. Control of trade offered by the charter allowed the Company jurisdiction within a two-mile radius of the city. It was their responsibility to monitor the quality, quantity and sales of fine saddlery, and the organization also offered apprenticeships for those entering the trade. Among the responsibilities of the Saddlers was the inspection of labour and pay conditions in the workplace. Anyone found breaching regulations would be brought before the Company

OPPOSITE *The awe inspiring Saddlers' Guild Hall in London.*

RIGHT *The majestic crest of the Worshipful Company of Saddlers.*

LEFT *The main entrance to the Saddlers' Hall, what would the Haunted Britain team discover?*

OPPOSITE *Two cameras are used at opposite ends of the room to capture known phenomena.*

Court and punishments ranging from fines to imprisonment were issued to those found guilty.

As was the case for many Livery Companies, the relaxation of trade and distribution laws from the 16th century onwards affected the Saddlers' hold over their profession. Laws were passed that allowed any Freeman of the City of London to follow the trade of their choice. This had a huge effect on the way the Livery Companies operated. London's high cost of living gradually forced tradesman out of the city in search of the cheaper resources found in more rural areas. Despite many pleas and requests to Parliament and the Corporation of London to restore the power once invested in them, the rights the Saddlers' Company held over its tradesmen waned.

By the 19th century the Saddlers' Company saw a decline in both the industry and its membership. Political groups fought to disband Livery Companies, with a view to returning full power to the manufacturers. The guilds fought valiantly to maintain their position and, after much debate, they were allowed to continue their work.

The threat of dissolution had a powerful effect on London's Livery Companies, including the Saddlers' Company, as it made them broaden their outlook. Along with many other guilds they helped to set up the City and Guilds of London Institute, which provides academic and vocational training within various professions. The Saddlers were among the founders of this popular educational enterprise, and by the beginning of the 20th century the Company was taking steps to benefit its own craft on a national scale.

THE INVESTIGATION BEGINS

This location was uncharted territory, as no paranormal investigation had been undertaken at the site before. Anxious as to what might be encountered, a meeting between Haunted Britain and the Company Beadle yielded no more clues. He remained tight-lipped, and gave nothing away.

From the moment the team stepped into the function rooms at Saddlers' Hall they experienced a welcoming atmosphere. Ornate ceilings and elegant furnishings imbue the site with grandeur and importance. You can almost feel yourself being transported into a very Victorian way of life, and can quite easily imagine a footman waiting in the plush hallway, just inside the front door, for the next important guest to arrive. As the investigation began, the building exuded this hospitable ambience, which was extremely calming, but there was much more to see. The team had yet to reach the hub of the paranormal activity.

'THEY'RE ALL HERE!'

The first room the team entered was a huge space that was usually divided into three smaller rooms separated by large wooden partitions. Opened up, this room spanned the length of the building. It was made up of the Livery Room, Court Room and Warden's Room (or anteroom). The group looked around, taking in the many fascinating items on display and absorbing the atmosphere. Moving into the Warden's Room at the far end, the Beadle turned to the team.

'They're all here,' he exclaimed, smiling warmly, 'and they're very happy to have you here for the evening.'

Who was here? And why are they happy to have the team present? The Beadle explained that during his time at the Company he had witnessed so much activity in the building and it occurred so regularly that the 'ghosts' that occupied the Saddlers' Hall had become like old friends. On the other hand, he had also hinted that not everyone in the hall would be as pleased to greet the group.

THE TUNNEL ROOM

Imposing is probably the first word that could describe the feeling within the Tunnel Room, or Saddlery. Beautiful is another, and spooky hits the nail on the head.

Even with the lights on, this room had a heavy and oppressive mood, and despite the light décor it felt incredibly dark and mysterious. Standing at the entrance, you could see why this was called the Tunnel Room. It was long and thin, and the perspective made it appear narrower at the far end.

The works of art on display relating to the saddlery trade astounded the team. The room was like a museum, exhibiting magnificent examples of the Company's skill. On one side of the room was an embroidered funeral pall, which was once used to cover the coffins of members of the Company. The team peered into the glass case containing this beautifully detailed cloth, but one of group stayed back. Something – or someone – was making it difficult for her to walk through this room.

The Beadle then confirmed that this was the room where he had experienced his most terrifying moment. Not giving too much away for the time being, the tour of Saddlers' Hall carried on. It was only later that the team discovered what had been seen here.

DANCING IN THE GREAT HALL

Venturing up a flight of stairs the team came to the Great Hall, which is the epitome of grace and elegance. A large, ornate chandelier glitters in the centre of this opulently decorated room, while portraits of some of the Company's benefactors and prominent members gaze down from the walls.

A complete contrast to the Tunnel Room, the Great Hall was extremely spacious. Above the fireplace was the large crest depicting the Company Arms and bearing the motto 'Hold

Fast, Sit Sure'. Nothing could have represented this organization's history and prestige more aptly.

Despite its size, the Great Hall has a very welcoming, effervescent atmosphere. This room is extremely atmospheric and conjures up a wealth of emotions and sensations, which excited the investigative team enormously.

'I feel like dancing,' laughed one of the team, and she held her arms up as though she was waltzing through the room. The rest of the team looked at her as though she was mad, but the Beadle smiled and said, 'I often get that impression too!'

The Great Hall is still frequently used as a function room for banquets and parties, so it was not unusual for it to be filled with dancing and frivolity. But why had sounds of festivities been heard when nobody was in the building? This phenomenon could be attributed to the Stone Wall Phenomena Theory (SWPT). Rather like a video recording, past feelings, emotions and atmospheres are imprinted on the room and replayed over and over again.

THE MINSTRELS' GALLERY

Leaving the opulence of the Great Hall behind for a short while, the tour continued. This was an extensive location and the group was anxious to get started with their research. But little did they know that the tour was going to take a dramatic turn.

Coming to yet another staircase, the team entered an area that was significantly less grand than the previous rooms. The gold decoration and luxurious red drapery had disappeared, and they entered surroundings that seemed more like an office building. An uncarpeted staircase and plainly painted walls lead to private areas that are used only by the Wardens, Masters and Officers of the company.

Just to the side of the staircase is a doorway leading to more stairs and down into a smaller room – the Minstrels' Gallery. Overlooking the Great Hall, this room is used, as its name suggests, by musicians during functions. At the back of the room are double doors that lead into the Beadle's flat. He told us that one night, while he was sleeping there, he was suddenly woken by a thunderous banging on the door, despite the fact that he was the only person in the building at the time. Hopefully, the Haunted Britain team would pick up something of the same phenomenon during their visit.

One possible reason for the Beadle's experience stems from the bombing raids of the Blitz. It would have been the

Beadle's job to ensure that the building was clear of residents, and evacuation procedures would have involved banging on the doors to alert anyone staying at Saddlers' Hall of the imminent danger. Could this be the type of imprinted memory that is typical of the SWPT (see pages 23–24)?

THE GUEST BEDROOM AND THE MYSTERY OF THE MOVING DOORSTOP

From the Minstrels' Gallery the team moved to a guest suite along the corridor. The room looks like a hotel bedroom, but there was a strange sense of oppression in the air and it felt very heavy and tense. It caused many impressions on the team and a few tension headaches were also suffered.

Two team members stood in the doorway. While listening to the discussions in the room they both heard a clicking noise, which sounded like a door handle being turned. The mechanism on the door had closed automatically and the only way to replicate the sound was by turning the handle. Was someone in the room with the team, or perhaps just leaving?

The team moved next door into a small conference room, the door to the bedroom closed behind them. Walking around the room the team agreed that it was relatively calm compared to room they had just left. As they were leaving, everyone heard a bang on the inside of the bedroom door.

There was nobody next door, as everyone was accounted for. Opening the door very slightly, the team peered inside. Behind the door a plastic door wedge lay on the floor. Careful not to move the doorstop three members of the group entered the room.

As the team had just left the room they would have seen or even kicked the wedge when they left. Also, as the door closed it would have pushed the doorstop out into the hall-way. If the wedge had been pushed out as the door was opened, how could have it had got there after the door had been closed? The loud bang against the door from the inside and the position of the object when re-entering the room was inexplicable and could have paranormal origins. Was someone trying to get the team's attention?

DEATH AND DIZZINESS IN THE CLERK'S OFFICE

The tour of Saddlers' Hall ended with an extremely strange emotional response from one of the team. On entering the Clerk's Office, one team member immediately felt very weak and unwell. The rest of the team moved further into the room, but she stayed near the door and sat down on a chair clutching her chest.

LEFT *The Minstrels' Gallery at the Worshipful Company of Saddlers was the site of inexplicable noises and bangs..*

'I feel so breathless and tight in my chest', she explained. Her medical history showed no history of chest or heart problems. Then she asked, 'did someone die in this room?'

'How did you know that?' the Beadle responded. 'That's not common knowledge.'

Although she had been to Saddlers' Hall before, she had no previous knowledge of the death in the Clerk's Office, as she had not been to this part of the building on her previous visit. Looking very pale and withdrawn, she described an elderly woman who had been in the room and died from heart problems. Astounded by her accuracy, the Beadle confirmed that a female guest staying in the bedroom adjacent to the Clerk's Office had died from a heart-related problem and was found some time later.

But it didn't end there. The bedroom looks more like a store cupboard and contains a pull-down bed, with a small toilet and kitchenette across a narrow hallway. The area has been the subject of many reports of paranormal activity.

Originally the Beadle's flat, the area had become the Clerk's Office and living quarters in more recent years. On many occasions the occupants of the bedroom have heard the loud jangling of a bunch of keys in the doorway followed by the sound of footsteps. They have also described the feeling of being watched over while in the bed, as well as fluctuations in temperature.

The team member who had felt ill joined the rest of the team in the flat, but instantly felt faint and physically sick. She was helped out of the room and taken back down stairs. She could not explain how she felt, but it was overwhelming. She would certainly not be joining any vigils in this room.

LOOKING FOR EVIDENCE

The Haunted Britain team were faced with a daunting task. Saddlers' Hall was an extensive location with a number of active areas to investigate.

Many visitors to the basement area had described the smell of decaying flesh and the stench of death. At this point, nobody but the Beadle knew about the ashes of a local vicar and his wife, which were kept in a store cupboard between the lift and the silver safe. Not wanting to draw too much attention to what was hidden, the Beadle remained silent.

The group made its way down to the basement. As they reached the last flight of stairs, a member of the team felt like she was being pushed from behind. Everyone else was either in front of her or out of reach.

But this visitor was not happy about what she sensed in the basement. When questioned as to why she was so hesitant to enter the room, she replied that two people were waiting for her down there. The Beadle replied that the room was empty, as all the staff had gone home – but she wasn't talking about the living.

'You've got two dead bodies down there. Please don't make me go down there!' she exclaimed

As you can imagine, the Beadle was astonished by her accuracy. Nobody knew about the ashes of the vicar and his wife, so there would have been no possible way that she could have knowledge of this information. Neither was she present as part of any type of paranormal investigation, she was merely a guest.

The Beadle has since removed his 'bodies' from the basement and reports of the pungent odour that had often been present have stopped.

The staff room in the basement made the perfect base for Haunted Britain's investigation, and the team split up to start their research. First on the agenda for one group was the large, integrated area that contained the Livery Room, Court Room and Warden's Room. The remaining members ventured back up to the guest suite.

TIME TO SIT AND WAIT

A large proportion of any investigation involves sitting and waiting for phenomena to occur. The bedroom had lost the oppressive feeling that the group had experienced during their first visit and it now appeared to be very calming and peaceful. Armed with a digital still camera and night-vision video camera, the team took their positions in chairs placed at the end of the bed. They started asking for any spirits present to make themselves known.

After a few minutes, an orb travelled across the bottom of the bed, moving away from the camera. The team member holding the camera witnessed this anomaly, and asked the spirits if they could do something again. A few more minutes passed and a second orb travelled from the camera towards the bed. The team also heard a loud click inside the bathroom. As nobody used this room during the day, it was unlikely to be the plumbing re-adjusting.

One member of the group decided to set up the doorstop as a trigger object. Setting it on the edge of the bedside table, she asked if the person who had moved it earlier was still present, and, if so, could they move the object again. She then lay on the bed and said that if they weren't

RIGHT *The Haunted Britain team delve deeper into the paranormal happenings at the Saddlers' Hall.*

happy for her to be there, they should let her know that she was not welcome.

Despite a few spirit lights photographed surrounding her on the bed, which cannot be ruled out as dust or reflective fragments from the soft furnishings, nothing else happened. Whatever had caused the earlier strange feelings in the room had departed. As the team left, it was decided to leave the doorstop to one side of the door. They checked it later in the evening, but were disappointed to discover that no movement had occurred.

MEANWHILE...

The team in the other rooms was experiencing much the same as the team in the bedroom. There was no escaping the fact that things at Saddlers' Hall had become eerily quiet. All the strange feelings that seemed to lurk around every corner while the lights were on, had, somewhat ironically, dissipated once the team were plunged into darkness. All was calm.

But the team didn't have to wait too long for activity to pick up. After about ten minutes one member of the group began to sense an increase in energy. She then asked politely for any spirits to try and communicate with her. Almost at once, a large, clearly defined orb moved across the front of the camera. Examination of the images taken of the orb ruled out the possibility of it being caused by insects or dust, due to its size and clarity. Digital photographs taken at this point also captured another bright-white light anomaly. It was uncharacteristic of the light anomalies usually recorded,

in that it was long and curved, rather than round in shape — almost as though it was moving. Again, examination of photographs ruled out any natural origin.

The temperature began to drop and the team sensed that something significant would eventually happen. They moved a camera to the edge of a table in the Warden's Room, facing into the centre of the Court Room. Once set up, they watched the footage on the screen.

Within seconds of repositioning the camera, a large, bright and unusually shaped light anomaly shot across the corner of the screen. What was even more peculiar was that it seemed to have a misty trail, which followed the contour of the main part of the light. Viewing the anomaly on the screen, the group alerted the other team. As the bedroom was proving very calm and quiet, they decided to join forces and move into the Tunnel Room.

Leaving a camera running in the Court Room, the group moved into the Tunnel Room. With everyone safely ensconced, the camera started to pick up a series of light anomalies moving backwards and forwards. There was no light source in the centre of the room to attract insects, nor was there any movement to stir up any dust particles. On viewing the footage, approximately 14 orbs were caught in this area, almost as though there was some kind of gathering. Had those who had come to welcome the team earlier in the visit made a brief reappearance?

LEFT *A light anomaly captured on digital camera, showing distinct movement and luminescence.*

OPPOSITE *A member of the Haunted Britain team sweeps for unusual EMF readings. Note the small light anomaly captured to the right.*

A BAD FEELING

Nervously, the team began its vigil in the Tunnel Room. One team member sat in a traditional upholstered armchair next to the glass case that contains the funeral pall. Another sat diagonally next to her. Everyone else was spread around the room.

Any location looks and feels different without the lights on, so it is important to allow enough time to let everything settle and for the senses to adjust, but it was obvious to everyone that something did not feel right in the Tunnel Room. Initial feelings were of oppression and sadness. With the lights on, this room had appeared overwhelming, its shape giving the impression of being enclosed. With no lights on and very limited vision, the Tunnel Room felt more like a cave.

Photographs revealed a few distinct orbs, particularly around the centre of the room. These rooms are meticulously cleaned, and the lack of dust was noticeable, although this doesn't completely discount the presence of airborne particles.

The team decided to ask the Beadle to try and open communication, as he had encountered the vision of a decomposing old woman here, an experience that had terrified him. As the team listened and watched for any responses to his questions, everyone noted that the atmosphere started to change. Two individuals complained of headaches and something seemed to be moving another team member's hair. She began to feel very uncomfortable and started feeling tiny shocks and prickling sensations in her hands. Although she was obviously unnerved, she chose to stay put, even though the sensations continued. Another member stood in the centre of the room and started to ask for the spirit to come forward. Someone else started to feel unwell and lay down on the floor, he felt as if he was being pushed down and he thought he couldn't stand or sit up without falling over. Concerned, the group asked if he was OK to continue the vigil. It was clear that feelings of pressure and oppression were escalating in the Tunnel Room.

Eventually the turmoil of emotions in the room became too much for one member and she left the room. The bizarre atmosphere had begun to take its toll on the team members – whoever haunted the Tunnel Room definitely wanted to make everyone feel as uncomfortable as possible. When asked why she felt the need to leave the vigil so abruptly, she replied that she felt like she was being toyed with and needed to get away from the oppressive atmosphere. As soon as she had removed herself from the area, the strange sensations she felt had stopped.

Could these odd feelings have been the decaying lady trying to make herself known? Things started to fall into

place. Then the members of the group that remained in the room noticed that three people were missing, so they went in search of them.

Two of the missing team members were found waiting in the corridor, the other one, who had felt so ill in the room, then came up the staircase looking extremely pale. It wasn't until this point that the team understood exactly how awful he had felt. He had needed to leave the room in order to cool down and had been physically sick. Whoever was haunting the Tunnel Room had certainly made a lasting impression on the Haunted Britain team.

KNOCK, KNOCK, WHO'S THERE?

After a short break the team split again. Armed with cameras, a dictaphone and an EMF Meter, two individuals headed off to the Minstrels' Gallery. The rest of the team occupied the Great Hall. It felt peculiar for two separate investigations to be conducted in such close proximity, as the groups were able to see each other, but it seemed to work well. After a period of asking questions individually, it was decided that one person should speak, as the acoustics in the Great Hall made it very difficult for noise within the two areas to be kept separate.

Even with the lights off, the Great Hall didn't feel at all ominous or spooky. However, there was still a feeling that the team was not alone. They asked for any spirits present to make themselves known. A few light anomalies started to appear, particularly around the double doors and near the chairs and tables. The group carried on filming and more light anomalies occurred, ranging from small flashing lights to large, moving orbs. As one member walked past the Beadle, she felt a cold rush of air pass her arm, as though something had walked into her.

The team tried asking for responses from two very prominent people in the Company's history, but nothing happened. A picture taken in this room many years earlier had revealed the image of a grand man wearing robes with what looked like an ermine collar. Unfortunately, it seemed that this person wasn't going to put an appearance in for the team.

The other group settled into the small gallery and started filming. They became very aware of noises emanating from the double doors leading to the Beadle's flat, and one of the team was convinced that he saw a light in front of the door when they entered the gallery. They started asking quietly for anyone present to communicate with them. After a few minutes, they heard a knocking sound coming from behind a stack of chairs near the doors.

Taking their cue from the team downstairs they waited for responses to their requests. Suddenly, one team member felt an urge to sit near the entrance door. His companion thought that he saw a shadow outside the door, but on turning towards the doorway, he discovered that there was nobody there. The top part of the door was made of glass, so it was easy to see if there was someone behind it. They immediately heard a large cracking sound coming from the ceiling above them — it was so loud that the team in the hall heard it. There was nobody upstairs, so they couldn't explain where this loud noise originated.

The team was about to end the vigil when they heard what sounded like footsteps in the corridor outside. Excited at the prospect of some activity, they asked for some further communication in the way of lights or physical contact. More small bangs and taps were heard, but this time the noises seemed to be coming from outside the gallery instead of inside. They decided to go and investigate the noises further, but nothing was found.

When the team checked the footage, they discovered that the knocks were accompanied by a few small light anomalies on the camera. The video footage also recorded a loud bang, which sounded like a heavy door slamming, and was not heard by either group. Again, all the team members were accounted for. It was also noted that all the doors near the Minstrels' Gallery were shut, propped open or locked, so, where could the noises have come from? The team will never know. What was apparent, was that things were starting to intensify.

THE BEADLE IS WATCHING YOU!

Moving away from the Minstrels' Gallery, the two members headed to the Clerk's Office. The feelings expressed there earlier had aroused much interest. Just because a person is known to have died in a room does not necessarily make it haunted. However, it is possible that such an event can leave a lasting impression and emotions in that area. As such, it was not just the unfortunate old lady that they were looking for. If she was still visiting the Saddlers' Hall, she would hopefully make herself known to the team.

But it was the ghost of a former Beadle that intrigued the group more than anything and they were anxious to

LEFT *The Main Hall and Minstrels Gallery within the Saddlers' Hall plays host to many forms of phenomena, including dinner parties in full swing.*

OPPOSITE *Even the smallest of rooms can be haunted.*

discover if the phenomenon of jangling keys and ghostly footsteps could be heard from inside the bedroom area. They started their vigil in the centre of the office and it didn't take long for things to start happening. One member began to feel hot, despite it being a relatively cool night. After a few requests for any spirits present to reveal themselves, the two heard footsteps that sounded as if they were coming up the staircase in the corridor.

At this point the rest of the team had moved to the basement, which was too great a distance for sounds to be heard on the second floor. It would have been impossible for the sound of footsteps to permeate through so many walls, closed doors and floors. If it wasn't one of the team, who was in the corridor?

A team member sat against the wall and suddenly felt a breeze engulf his arm, which made his hair stand on end. He held his hand out and at first the air felt warm. He asked whoever was in the room to make his hand go cold. Almost immediately this happened. When he moved his hand, it warmed up. This temperature change was confirmed by his team-mate and the infrared thermometer.

The pair moved into the small flat where they set up a camera in the doorway to face the bed. One of the team climbed on the bed, the other moved into the kitchen. Almost instantly, there seemed to be a visitor in the bedroom. The person on the bed sat up and asked if someone was there with him. He looked towards the door – his eyes wide and extremely alert. He stood by the camera and saw an orb travel across the side of the bed. Just then both men heard noises and made their way into the corridor. One team member had heard something in the corridor that sounded like a door banging shut. But the team member in the bedroom had heard something different, something closer – a shuffling sound in the hallway. The pair moved back in to the office and contacted the rest of the team to confirm that they were still in the basement. Unknown to both of them, the camera was picking up what they had wanted to hear.

Looking at the footage later, an orb travelled across the bed. Even more exciting, while the two men were talking in the office, a clear jangling of keys could be heard. The team's pockets were empty and no-one was near the camera. A second and louder jangling appeared to occur right next to the camera, drowning out other noises. It seemed that someone had finally wanted to confirm their presence, and it supported previous claims of experiencing the same phenomena.

SUMMARY OF THE INVESTIGATION

Saddlers' Hall is undoubtedly shrouded in history and the building appears to have experienced many signs of paranormal activity, a few of which the Haunted Britain team also witnessed. The site is definitely worth further investigation, as there seems to be much more waiting to reveal itself.

All in all, this is a beautiful location with a very warm and welcoming atmosphere, which can soon change when the lights go out. There are many spirits that haunt the hall for different reasons. Some seem friendly, but others are not so hospitable, and without a doubt these beings can, and do, make themselves known.

THE TALBOT INN
4 THURCASTON ROAD, LEICESTER, LE4 5PF

THE LOCATION AND ITS HISTORY

Buried deep in the heart of Leicester and the heart of the infamous Belgrave Triangle lies The Talbot Inn. The Belgrave triangle came to light in December 1998, when a strange image was captured on the CCTV Cameras at Belgrave Hall, the image only lasts for around two seconds but seems to be that of a figure standing in the gardens.

Many people have seen the photographs taken, and many have arrived at the conclusion of a leaf blowing in the shot originally triggered by a wild animal or cat. The mist running along the back wall however, still remains a topic of much debate. Could it be a car exhaust (considering there are no roads that side of the gardens), a spider very close to the lens, or something paranormal? The debate continues.

The events that transpired in 1998 opened the door of Belgrave Hall, and allowed different investigators to visit including the famous ISPR team (including a young Derek Acorah). During their investigation, the ghosts of Belgrave

ABOVE The Talbot Inn is said to be one of the UK's most haunted public houses. Reports of paranormal phenomena date back to Victorian times.

Hall made themselves known to the team and the world watched as the history of Belgrave Hall unravelled before their eyes.

Ghost sightings at Belgrave Hall have seemingly been a very common occurrence; one of the gardeners swears he encountered a woman dressed in Victorian clothing walking down the stairs. It is said that she stopped, turned to look at him, smiled and then vanished into the kitchen. Inspections of the kitchen were carried out and nothing was found.

This, it seems, was just the tip of the iceberg for the Belgrave Triangle.

Next door to Belgrave Hall lies Belgrave Church, and its cemetery. During routine work bones were uncovered buried in what looked like a mass burial pit. They were re-interred but since that time visitors and paranormal investigators to the area have reported strange phenomena at work, including orbs, noises and ghostly apparitions.

The Talbot Inn seemed to remain out of the picture.

From its original inception the inn used to host paying guests as they travelled through Leicester and near outlying villages of the north. During these times, all people would have had to pass the Talbot Inn on their way to the toll bridge and the city.

Travellers and locals alike would use the Talbot Inn as a hostelry, and as Loughborough Road did not exist: all villains would pass the Talbot on their way to the gallows. Most villains intended for the gallows would be allowed a final drink at the Talbot Inn, to sum up enough 'Dutch courage' for their final journey. Once the deed had been done, the bodies were then taken back to the Talbot Inn, where the outbuildings were used as a rudimentary morgue.

There are two cellars in the Talbot Inn, but only one is in use today. The other has been bricked up. The main cellar runs under the lounge bar, and is split into two types of stonework. The front part is ancient, and certainly would have

formed part of the original structure; it can be dated between the 11th and 12th centuries. The second cellar runs along the front, under the bar area – it was possibly used by the servants and licensee as their living accommodation.

In the late 1950s a fire raged through the Talbot Inn and in 1958 the local authorities granted the inn a sum of money for repairs. This was when the third floor was removed. From that point, the Talbot Inn no longer took paying guests.

The building you see is only a few hundred years old and has had considerable alterations over the years. The main cellar now stores cask ales, and there are arches in the walls which are bricked up ... these may be tunnels or priest holes. It is rumoured that these tunnels could lead to Belgrave Hall and the nearby Church.

Numerous paranormal investigators and members of the general public have witnessed striking apparitions in the Talbot Inn and we have so far collected the following information about the ghosts that seem to be inhabiting this fantastic building:

RIGHT *A young boy has been seen on many occasions at the fireplace, so a locked–off camera was used to try and capture any sight of him.*

1. The figure of a lady has been seen walking through the false wall late at night, she has long flowing hair and is commonly named as Hairy Mary. There was a Mary Dawson who had six children and was at one time the landlady of the pub. It is also worthy of note that a lot of the staff at The Talbot Inn will not enter the cellar alone.

2. The figure of a small boy has been seen by a previous occupant, in the fireplace of the lounge. He was sitting on a stool, swinging his legs and smiling. He has also been seen in the cellar by the same person.

3. The face of a man has been seen through the window at the back of the lounge, he was said to have a heavily disfigured face.

4. A shimmering figure was seen by a previous landlady as she did some gardening, on the border outside (next to the car park). It was the height of a small man and moved slightly. The landlady had been warm, but went cold and was unable to move through fear. It vanished very quickly.

5. A man has been seen several times by two separate landlords. The man appears by the bar wearing an old caped raincoat, he carries an old leather purse and is said to open it and search for a few coins before walking through the wall to his left. Although he was seen to walk through the wall, this was the entrance before the pub alterations.

6. On several occasions, noises have been heard from upstairs when the flat has been empty.
   Please be aware, that before an investigation only a few key team members are given the facts about the reported sightings. On this occasion however, no member of the team was given prior information or knowledge about the ghosts, apparitions and sightings.

LEFT *The snug at the Talbot Inn played host to many gallows victims prior to their hanging.*

OPPOSITE *The dark and foreboding cellar of the Talbot Inn. The figure of a young boy has also been seen here. Many of the staff at the inn will not enter the cellar alone.*

THE INVESTIGATION BEGINS

The team entered the Talbot Inn and were given a guided tour of the building by the landlord and landlady. Baseline tests were taken and any unusual cold spots, lights and other phenomena were recorded to provide a constant from which to work from. Almost immediately it was noted than one particular section of the Main Bar was a lot colder than everywhere else, and so a note was made to investigate this thoroughly later on in the evening.

One of the members was taken downstairs into the cellar and shown the possible dangers of conducting an investigation in these dark and cramped conditions. However due to the historical nature of the cellar it was agreed that an investigation would be imperative and that nobody should enter the cellar alone.

With the baseline tests completed and the team ready to being their investigation, the lights were turned off and the team split into two groups.

NO SOONER HAD WE SPOKEN...

Half of the Haunted Britain team opened the door to the cellar and descended into the oldest part, one of the remaining members stood at the top of the door and as soon as the team members became comfortable (if that was possible) the lights were turned off.

Meanwhile, the remainder of the team sat in the Main Bar and began to investigate the cold spot that had been noticed earlier. It seemed that nothing was causing it, as the air conditioning was at the other end of the room, and the radiator was the only temperature changing device located in the vicinity – and the radiator had been on all night.

Suddenly, the team members in the Main Bar heard the most blood curdling scream. A scream that seemed to describe utter panic and fear. They ran towards the cellar and precariously turned the light on and descended down the stairs.

They were greeted with the sight of a team member in tears, visibly shaken and distraught at what had just transpired, and so the lights were turned on and the team member began to describe what had happened in her own words.

'I had turned around to look at the old archways that could possibly have been tunnels, and turned back to see somebody that I thought was a team member standing right in front of me – staring at me!

It took me a few moments to realise that it wasn't a member of the team, and then panic kicked in and I screamed. At the moment I did, whatever it was vanished.'

When asked for a description of what she had just seen, the following was given:

'She had a strange blue glow, which at first I thought was a torch. Her hair was lank and matted over her face and she was staring at me through the tops of her eyes. As if to say that we weren't wanted there.'

Obviously upset at what had just happened, it was decided that a break was in order and the team sat and discussed what had happened and watched the video footage back of the cellar vigil, unfortunately nothing had been captured on video camera and no photographs were taken in the cellar.

What had happened down there had changed the way a member of the Haunted Britain team felt ... in her own words ...

'I will never forget what I saw, for weeks after the event I closed my eyes and all I could see was her face staring at me. It is hard to describe but I used to be one of the people who said that they really wanted to see a ghost ... believe me you don't.'

THE INVESTIGATION CONTINUES

After an extensive break and recovery period, the team decided to conduct investigations as a complete unit and re-entered the Main Bar to try and quantify any source of paranormal activity.

The group took various positions around the bar and allowed the room to settle before the investigation continued.

The room is allowed to settle for a number of reasons, both theoretic and based in common sense.

If a room is haunted, and the spirits are known to be active, then it seems to be common sense to allow the spirits in the room (if they exist) to become accustomed to our presence. Also we allow the room to settle so that any dust or other airborne particles that we may have disturbed, are allowed to settle and not to taint any photographs we may take.

After around 20 minutes of waiting, the group began to ask questions to the possibility of a spirit or ghost. Unfortunately it seemed that nothing wanted to communicate with us, and the trigger objects that we had set had not moved in the slightest.

The group left the Main Bar and proceeded to the Lounge Bar.

THE LOUNGE BAR AND THE LITTLE BOY

The team entered the Lounge Bar and sat themselves at different positions, and followed the usual routine of allowing the room to settle. However one member of the group was drawn towards the fireplace and took a new seat.

The rest of team began to take photographs and noticed that the team member at the fireplace seemed to be crying. The member of the team was obviously upset and is not normally a member of the team that would be upset at anything.

He described his experience as:

'Bizarre, it was really bizarre. Even though I had my eyes closed I could see a little boy sitting on the brass stool, looking very upset. He seemed to be saying that he wanted to leave this place but didn't know how to get out, and didn't know how he got there in the first place. Nothing has ever upset me like that before, this was just weird!'

A strange point of note is that as soon as that team member left the stool near the fireplace, he returned to his normal composure and looked like he hadn't been crying at all. Could this have been paranormal?

During this experience, the room had also lowered in temperature. This was noticed by all members that were present, however it had not been picked up on any of the equipment that was recording during the vigil.

So who goes into the cellar now?

It seems a sorry state of affairs when paranormal investigators are too afraid to enter a haunted room. However (we are sorry to say) that this was the case we were left with. Some of the team members now refused to enter the cellar after what had happened there earlier.

A member of the team opened the door and the rest of the group looked down into the seeming abyss. Almost as soon as one member looked he felt something scrape along his back. Shocked, he stepped back and asked the team to look for anything that could have caused this sensation.

Upon lifting his shirt it was noted that there were two visible scratch marks along the bottom of his back, which seemed to disappear very quickly until there was almost nothing left.

Two brave members of the group then decided to enter the basement to conduct a follow-up investigation. They descended with a certain degree of trepidation, however this was uncalled for as throughout their investigation nothing occurred.

The second investigation

Following the enormity of the results of the Haunted Britain team's first investigation, it was decided that a second was in order. And so the team re-entered the Talbot Inn, and took their initial baseline tests.

It was noted on that evening that the pub had a lighter atmosphere than was anticipated. The group had a unnerving

sense of fear and anticipation following the results of the previous investigation, and so with some trepidation, they began to wait for the pub to clear of its residents (hopefully not those of the non-living persuasion).

OFF THE SCALE READINGS IN THE LOUNGE!

After the pub had cleared, the Haunted Britain team decided to conduct their first investigation in the Lounge Bar. Trigger objects of Victorian coins were set up on the stool belonging to the small boy who sits by the fireplace, some were also set up around the stool (just in case).

The team then started filming and photographing the room and quickly it was noticed that a small alcove was giving high EMF readings. The group checked with the landlord and landlady, and no wiring was running above the alcove. However as the EMF Meter was raised towards the ceiling, the readings started to go off the scale in one location.

The team decided to keep the EMF Meter in that specific location, and notes and readings were taken over a 30 minute period. During this time the EMF Meter began to fluctuate, and it was noted that the readings dropped and rose at differing intervals.

BELOW *High EMF readings were captured in the main bar of the Talbot Inn, in an area with no power cables. As soon as the readings were taken, they dropped down to zero.*

A group decision was made to begin asking questions, using the EMF Meter as a form of communicator.

'If there is anybody present, excluding the members of the group, who wishes to talk to us, we have a machine here that we can use to talk with you. If you wish to answer a question or respond to our request please move closer to the machine making the noise. If you do not wish to answer, or the answer is no, please move away from the machine.'

Almost immediately, the EMF Meter began making a louder and higher pitched noise. As if it had just been passed by a plug socket. Almost as soon as the team had noticed the increase in noise, it disappeared leaving nothing but a small buzz from the machine.

'If there is somebody there, would you like to leave us a message?'

The faint buzz still emanated from the EMF Meter, unfortunately it did not raise in reading at all.

'Are you afraid of us?'

Again, there was no increase in readings from the EMF Meter, and so a different tack was chosen to attempt to establish communication between the Haunted Britain team and whatever inhabits the Talbot Inn.

'Again, if there is somebody in this room with us, excluding members of the team, please could you walk closer to the machine making the noise'

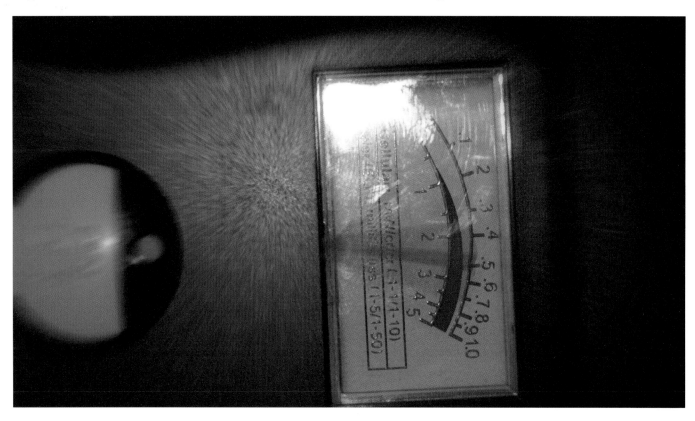

The EMF Meter shot into life, hitting its maximum reading. The noise came as a shock to most of the group, as results of this nature are not expected immediately. The high readings continued …

'Now, will you please move away from the machine'

The EMF Meter began to lower in tone and pitch signifying that an Electro Magnetic Field was moving away from the group (who had remained stationary for the entire vigil).

'Again please move closer to the machine'

Before the question could be completed the machine began to raise in tone and pitch again. However it did not reach the peak that was recorded on the previous effort. A noticeable difference on this occasion was that the EMF Meter did not remain constant and it seemed like the Electro Magnetic Field moved away slowly.

From this point onwards the EMF Meter gave normal readings in the alcove of the Talbot Inn.

However a member of the team captured a slow moving orb on camera, moving towards and away from the alcove where the remainder of the team was located. Could this have been a sign that there was 'something' there with the group? We will never know!

IS THERE SOMEBODY SITTING NEXT TO ME?

The team then moved on from the Lounge Bar, into the Main Bar, and immediately set up the skittles on the table as a form of trigger object. This was due to an apparition that had been seen by the skittles table, and if they were in some way interconnected the trigger object would prove very useful.

The team then took different positions around the room, and allowed the atmosphere to settle before asking questions to the possibility of a ghost or spirit. Baselines were taken during this period, it was noted that one wall was significant-

ABOVE *One of the team members began to feel very ill during the investigation. As soon as he left the room – the feelings disappeared.*

ly colder than the others, but this was due to three large windows that it contained. Nothing unusual was noted during the baseline tests and so the team began to investigate the Main Bar for the second time.

A member of the team sat against the outer wall, and immediately reported the feeling of somebody sitting next to them. They described it as:

'Very strange, I just felt like there was somebody I didn't know sitting very closely next to me. I kept having to look at that spot, just to convince myself that nothing was there.'

Unfortunately during the second investigation into the Main Bar, no other strange phenomena occurred. Various questions were asked, and the EMF Meter was used as a method of communication again, all yielded little or no results. With time pressing on the group decided that a small break was in order before they ventured into the now infamous cellar.

BACK INTO THE DARKNESS!

After a small break, and a much needed cup of coffee, the team decided to enter the basement for the second time, and to include the original member who saw the terrifying apparition. One member of the group remained at the top of the stairs in charge of the lighting, and the other three descended the stairs, disappearing one by one into the seeming abyss below.

The member of the team who had seen the apparition last time was very tense and nervous but did not report any feelings of anything like she endured on the previous investigation.

Shortly after arriving in the cellar, one member of the team reported being kicked in the leg. He described the feeling as similar to being kicked by a child, however, on all video footage there is nobody near him at the time of the incident. The impact seemed very low down, and very low powered. It also seemed as if whoever kicked him, had ran past him after the incident.

Upon further research it transpired that the ghost of a young boy has been seen in the basement, and has been known to be quite mischievous with regards to other people and paranormal investigators at the Talbot Inn, could this have been him?

Another point of note is that the cellar at the Talbot Inn is black. You can hold you hand just in front of your face and not see a thing. The pumps and other mechanisms working down there also give off an awful lot of noise, so with two of your senses depleted all paranormal investigators who have visited the Talbot Inn Cellar have described it as an unnerving experience to say the least!

LEFT *The wall which Mary is said to walk through. It is said that a tunnel runs from here to Belgrave Hall and the church nearby.*

SUMMARY OF THE INVESTIGATION

If there is such a thing as a haunted pub or inn, the Talbot Inn is it! Bearing stonework from the 11th and 12th Centuries the pub has stood the test of time and seemingly brought previous occupants along for the ride.

Never before have we investigated a pub twice, and we still feel that the Talbot Inn deserves a more in-depth analysis; the evidence we have captured is testament to this.

During our first investigation, the team were shocked when we looked at the photographic evidence. It seems we have captured the striking image of a face looking at one of the members in the dark. The face is glowing (or so it seems) bright orange and the video footage of this investigation does not show any strange lights or anomalous phenomena that could tie in with this strange photograph.

Various people have seen the photograph, and always on every explanation we never offer a description but simply ask them what it looks like, and so far 100 per cent of people asked have described it as being the face of a disfigured man. We can then tie this in to one of the ghosts seen regularly in the Talbot Inn... the face of a man has been seen through the window at the back of the lounge, he was said to have a heavily disfigured face.

Take a look at the photograph and see what you think!?

Now we move on to the apparition that was witnessed in the basement on our first investigation. When asked about this we always describe the scream as 'that type of scream, when you know something is wrong!', there was something in the scream that signalled that the team member had seen something horrific, and the reaction that was witnessed was the most horrific of all. The team member could not sleep for several days after the event, and when the team discovered the photograph of the glowing face, the team member began to get very upset with the 'all too real' aspect of the investigation.

That team member originally began as a very sceptical investigator, that one experience has now changed her perspective totally to one of believing in ghosts and the paranormal.

Overall the Talbot Inn (Leicester) is probably one of the strangest locations we have ever visited. Nestled deep within the Belgrave triangle, the strange occurrences still continue to this day ... simply ask a member of staff!

RIGHT *A strange face captured on the wall by digital camera. The image has only been lightened very slightly. No explanation has been found to this day.*

THE GALLERIES OF JUSTICE
HIGH PAVEMENT, THE LACE MARKET, NOTTINGHAM, NG1 1HN

PREVIOUS SIGHTINGS

- Shadows and footsteps in the courtyard
- Strange voices
- Cold spots
- Orbs and other light anomalies
- Doors banging
- Strange smells
- Objects moving of their own accord
- Feelings of depression, sadness, and of being watched

THE LOCATION

Nottingham's Galleries of Justice is perhaps one of the most famous of Britain's haunted buildings. The numerous ghostly sightings, strange noises and unusual phenomena reported from the site have prompted many investigators to label the former prison as one of the country's most active paranormal locations. With a history that stretches back to the 18th century, the site is replete with tales of terror, torture and death, and the Haunted Britain team just had to investigate this amazing location.

Tucked away in a winding side street in Nottingham's Lace Market area, the Shire Hall, now known as the Galleries of Justice, has served as a legal stronghold since the 1780s and many of the county's less law-abiding citizens were housed here.

When the Court House was first erected, it sat proudly among small local businesses and factories and all who passed it would have respected its stature and importance. Today the building is surrounded by a host of bars, restaurants and bustling nightclubs, and it is highly unlikely that many of the city's nightly revellers even realize the significance of the site or what is housed beneath it.

Intimidating iron gates at the side of the building lead into a small cobbled courtyard. When the building was a working prison, this entrance would have been used to bring inmates into the jail, and once those gates were shut, it was the last time many saw civilization. Little did these unfortunate souls know what awaited them inside, for below the surface of the imposing mansion-style exterior, with its towering white-stone pillars and large, bracing front doors, lies a dark and chilling glimpse into what life was like for those caught breaking the law in times past. And from the reports and stories recounted by many visitors and workers at the Galleries of Justice, Haunted Britain's journey through the building would not be one that they made alone.

THE HISTORY

It is believed that the plot the Galleries of Justice occupies has been the site of a court since 1375 and a prison since 1449. It is possible that many of the caves and sandstone cells date back to this period. However, the building on view today was constructed in the 1780s. It was used as a prison until the 1980s and it has held prisoners from some of the country's most high-profile cases.

The building was, for many who walked through its doors, a place of fear and immense terror. The steps that lead to the front doors were once the setting for public executions. Once the thirst for the gruesome sight of these deaths had dissipated, executions took place inside the prison, until the 1960s, when capital punishment was abolished. For those unlucky enough to be sentenced to death, this place would be their last living memory. From the moment their sentence was passed they were taken down into the cells, where they were held until their day of reckoning.

In the 19th century, prisoners were not entitled to anything but shackles and a blanket. Anything else was purchased from the jailers. Prisoners with no money had to barter their wares for basic food and supplies, or they would go hungry and freeze in their cells. Other inmates would occasionally have taken pity on the less affluent and shared their possessions, but such geniality was rare.

THE INVESTIGATION BEGINS

Inside the building are two contrasting areas, splitting the Galleries of Justice into distinct sections. The first part of the building is the Court House. It has two court rooms, one was used for civil cases and the other for more high-profile criminal cases. The latter is where many convicted criminals were sentenced to death. The courts are not used today, but form part of a museum and are sometimes used for filming.

The upper floors of the Galleries of Justice are clean, warm and functional. Everything about this part of the building feels very official and wealthy. Carpeted floors, white furnishings and walls decorated with gold and brass embellishments offer a total contrast to what waited for

BELOW *One of the cells which would house the condemned at the Galleries of Justice. From the moment their sentence was passed they were taken down into the cells, where they were held until execution. Many ghosts and spirits have been seen in the cells.*

prisoners downstairs. Mugshots Café is also in this part of the building and the upper floors are home to a wealth of offices and meeting rooms. This was to be the team's base for their evening investigation.

Below what you would be mistaken to think of as ground level, the prison area of the building begins.

THE RECEPTION HALL AND ENTRANCE

The reception area and entrance hall are grand and rather daunting. It is difficult to forget that this area is used as a museum, as a large amount of promotional material abounds. It is also home to a rather lifelike figure of what is either a jailer or a prisoner. It was hard, as we entered the building, to shake the sensation of being watched. The longer we stared at this figure, the more we seemed to be waiting for it to move. Would this set the precedent for the investigation?

Given the strange sensations felt in this room, the group began to investigate. The team later discovered that a photograph taken some years earlier had shown a ghostly figure walking down the staircase into the room. The figure had also been witnessed by many other people.

The atmosphere settled, and the group asked questions, hoping to catch sight or sound of something or someone

out of the ordinary. Unfortunately, nothing seemed to occur, and so they moved on.

THE WALK OF THE CONDEMNED

From the dock in the main court room, a stairwell leads down to the first part of the cells. A wide corridor with a stone wall leads through the museum displays into the jailer's office. Thick, iron-barred gates separate the corridor from the cells, giving the firm impression that the inhabitants of these rooms were locked away from society.

After a brief talk by our guide, who explained what conditions were like in the prison and described the ghastly role of a Victorian jailer, the team moved into the holding cell, which was where prisoners were taken from the court room. During the period that the cells were in use, they were crammed with many different types of felon, from murderers to thieves and petty criminals — all of whom were treated in the same way.

The group sat quietly on the floor of the cell and allowed the atmosphere to settle, as they had done in the previous room. Within the space of a few moments, an air of oppression gripped the team, and many members reported the feeling that they were being watched. They began to

record the scene with dictaphones. One team member asked if any spirits were present, and requested that they leave a message on the machine that he was holding. Almost as soon as the question was asked, the sound of shuffling could be heard in the corridor, and the team jumped to investigate the possible cause. The door was opened gently, but an empty corridor greeted the group. Could the sound have been paranormal? We will never know.

The group returned to the cell and the atmosphere calmed down. The dictaphone began to record again, and the same team member asked if the spirit of the jailer was present and if he could open the cell door for the group. Unfortunately, the plea yielded no results.

Shortly afterwards, another member of the team started to feel like her hair was being touched. She described the sensation – it was as if somebody was running their fingers through her hair from the crown of her head to the nape of her neck. As she revealed this unnerving feeling, it seemed to stop. It is worth mentioning at this point, that due to the cramped conditions we were not able to qualify the evidence taken in the room, as an overwhelming feeling of incarceration loomed over the entire team, and this sort of feeling could play tricks with even the most hardened of paranormal investigators.

The group sat together in the cell for a further 20 minutes, and no further phenomena seemed to occur. Thanking any spirits that had attempted to communicate, the group left the cell and headed towards the system of caves that had recently been discovered underneath the building.

THE NEW CAVES

The group headed deep beneath the Galleries of Justice, moving to a location that had only been discovered when a workman fell through the floor and landed in what was revealed to be an ancient chapel. The entire group stayed together in these cramped conditions, sitting along the length of the chapel, opposite the altar and a cross that had been placed there as a trigger object. However, this had not seemed to move since it was installed.

After letting the ambience settle down, the group heard the sounds of dragging footsteps emanating from the corridors outside. One team member leapt up to find the possible cause, only to find an empty corridor, but he had the distinct impression that somebody, or something, had been listening to the activity in the chapel.

The walls of the old chapel did not help the sense of dread that began to overtake the team. Red lamps shone from the

ABOVE *Trigger objects pertaining to the ghosts and spirits said to haunt the location are used to try and record interaction. It is important to use objects which will be recognizable to the ghosts and spirits, otherwise they are unlikely to be effective.*

OPPOSITE *A friend of Haunted Britain was filmed with a strange white rope around her neck whilst standing on the gallows. This light disappeared very quickly, and cannot be explained.*

ceiling, casting an eerie glow and forming strange shapes, as if trying to capture the team's imaginations and strengthen the feeling that somebody was watching the group.

A team member began to ask questions, asking if any spirit present could please come forward and interact with the group. Shortly afterwards, more noises were heard in the corridor, but upon investigation nothing was found.

Feeling rather overwhelmed by the gloomy chapel, the group descended into another cave that had recently been excavated. A pile of earth and sandstone greeted the team, and as their eyes began to adjust to the darker surroundings they realized the true nature of where they were standing. The cavern was enormous, stretching back as far as the team could see. Standing in this ominous section of the Galleries of Justice, the team huddled together, unwilling to stand with their backs to what seemed like an abyss.

The room contained copious amounts of dust, grit and other airborne particles that were used to try and create orbs.

The group threw dust into the air and tried to photograph the descending particles, but when the film and digital stills were studied later no light anomalies were present.

Shortly after this experiment, every member of the team heard what could only be described as the sound of heavy shuffling feet. The mysterious sound came from an area that seemed even blacker than the rest of the cavern – the area that the team had just come from. A member of the group raced to sit alone in the tunnel, but unfortunately, despite asking numerous questions of any spirits present and requesting some form of interaction with whatever was hiding in the shadows, nothing happened. The team moved on once again.

THE COURTYARD

The group left the cave system, ascended the walk of the condemned and made their way to the courtyard. This had been the prison's place of execution, and it was also where inmates were allowed a meagre amount of exercise. The high walls surrounding the courtyard seemed to block the light from entering certain areas of the yard, and some small alleyways were almost pitch black. Standing prominently at the end of the yard were the infamous gallows.

A member of the team sat at the top of the steps, while the rest of the group sat below. Because the team was now outside, no EVP could be counted as evidence, as the noise of the bustling city of Nottingham was just over the wall.

One member of the group decided to stand near the gallows. Then, a strange thing occurred, a white line appeared around her neck that seemed to link itself to the rope that was hanging behind her. Whenever she moved, so did the white line. We set about conducting experiments to find out if the white line was a trick of the light, or a reflection. What proved bizarre about this phenomenon was that when the line was covered, it disappeared, which discounted any form of light reflection. Could this apparition be the spirit of somebody hanged here, or possibly a hangman trying to communicate with us?

When the group gathered around the gallows to observe this peculiar incident, the white line seemed to vanish. It was not seen on any other member of the group brave enough to stand around the gallows.

Next the team proceeded along a long alleyway that led off from the main exercise yard. The high walls and confined spaces conveyed a feeling of oppression, and it was felt that something or somebody was waiting for the team at the end of the corridor.

At the end of the long, black corridor was a high, gated door. Looking down, the team could see the bustling city of Nottingham below. It transpired that this door was used to sneak objects and also people through the Galleries of Justice. Despite many attempts at communication, no further phenomena were recorded or felt.

THE MAIN COURT ROOM

As the team walked back into the main court room to conduct the biggest vigil of the evening, they were joined by an individual who claimed to be a medium. Adding this member to the investigative team, the group entered the large room, each member sitting at a different location in order to cover the vast space. Some members of the group sat around the main table, below the Judge's chair. The medium instantly started to feel very angry. She described a feeling of frustration, of being told something but not being able to do anything about it.

This could have been a psychic emanation. However, it is common knowledge that many of those who visited this room to be tried would never see the outside world again. Some of these unfortunates could have been scapegoats — guilty of nothing at all. As soon as the medium began describing this phenomenon, three team members saw what appeared to be an orb floating down from the ceiling and

LEFT *The harsh and brutal tools of the Galleries' doctor.*

OPPOSITE *The corridors of the Galleries of Justice are equally as haunted as the cells themselves. During the investigation one team member asked if any spirits were present, and requested that they leave a message on the machine that he was holding. Almost as soon as the question was asked, the sound of shuffling could be heard in the corridor.*

past the Judge's chair. This light anomaly was caught on both digital and film cameras.

It is worth noting that the court contains some rather lifelike dummies of officials and watchers. In these situations, the mind can definitely play tricks and the dummies could have made the team feel more susceptible to feelings of being watched. However, nobody on the team described this sensation – what were experienced were feelings of sheer frustration and upset.

THE CIVIL COURT

The team then moved from the main court room to the Civil Court. Before the visit by Haunted Britain, a medium had described the same feelings that our medium began to describe on entering this room. The individuals that work at the Galleries of Justice were confused by what the medium had said, as they were not aware that this room had been used to deal severe punishments. With gusto, the team set about to research what the medium had revealed.

It transpired that due to massive overflow problems, criminals were tried, convicted and put to death in this room, and so the psychic medium had predicted something that was correct – before the staff at the Galleries of Justice had known anything about it.

Unfortunately, despite numerous attempts to try and contact any spirits in the room, nothing happened. The group remained calm and united, but still nothing. A total of 30 minutes was spent trying to communicate with spirits in the Civil Court and not once did a member of the team report any strange sensations or phenomena.

And so … the team moved onwards.

THE WASHROOM

The team descended back down the walk of the condemned and made their way to the ladies' washroom. The room is quite large and features much that has stood the test of time and is still on display today. These items include a small bath, a fumigation screen and three offices used by members of staff.

One of these offices belonged to the 'surgeon' – a term that is best used loosely, as this individual's methods of operating often involved the unnecessary loss of a limb or two.

The team entered the room to be greeted by the stale smell of carbolic soap. Taking their places around the perimeter of the room, the group attempted to communicate with any spirits present in this location. During this process, members of the team reported headaches, backaches and feelings of oppression and discomfort. Were these sensations due to the nature of the room's previous function? Or were they simply feelings that were embedded in the minds of the team?

Again, no visible or audible phenomena were captured in the washroom, and the team moved next door to the ladies' bedroom.

THE LADIES' BEDROOM

The stark surroundings of the ladies' bedroom conveyed the atrocious conditions that the previous inhabitants were made to suffer. The bed was rock hard and 16 clothes pegs were mounted on the walls – did this many poor women share this space?

The team sat at different points around the room, some on the bed, some on the benches and some on the floor. Almost immediately, one member reported that she felt labour pains and recounted feelings of depression and mourning. It seemed that many similar emotions were being conveyed to the female members of the team. Others felt as though they were pregnant or miscarrying. The atmosphere within the room seemed to change in an instant. It was decided to conduct a séance.

Sitting in a circle upon the floor, the team took a moment to take some psychic protection, and after a few quiet moments and prayers, began to ask questions. The séance lasted for 35 minutes, but, unfortunately, no audible or visible phenomena were captured. However, the pains, aches and general feelings of sorrow were enhanced.

It was decided that the female members of the team should leave the room, just in case anything serious happened to one of them. And so the men were left alone in the ladies' bedroom! Despite the presence of these two handsome chaps, no phenomena were recorded here.

SUMMARY OF THE INVESTIGATION

The Galleries of Justice is an impressive location to say the least, and it subjected the team to a series of emotional and physical episodes. By far the greatest piece of evidence gathered here was the apparent apparition of a rope around the neck of one of the team members. This video has been scrutinized by a series of individuals, who offered the following explanations.

The first explanation is that the light around this individual's neck was some form of reflection, emanating from an undisclosed light source. However, no torches were taken outside and the only lights that entered the courtyard were from the distant nightlife of Nottingham. The second possible explanation for the phenomenon is that it was a parnormal manifestation of a rope around her neck.

All in all, the evening spent at Nottingham's Galleries of Justice proved to be an excellent investigation – and the Haunted Britain team will certainly be going back to capture more fascinating evidence.

GRACE DIEU PRIORY
THRINGSTONE, LEICESTERSHIRE

PREVIOUS SIGHTINGS AND EXPERIENCES

- A ghostly woman in white
- Strange noises, especially squeaking
- Children's cries
- Footsteps

THE LOCATION AND ITS HISTORY

In the north west of Leicestershire, lies Grace Dieu Priory. It is a place of legend, where children fear to tread as the result of tales of 'the White Lady', peculiar noises and many other strange occurrences. The priory is maintained by the Grace Dieu Trust, a charity that is dedicated to raising money for the site to keep its heritage alive.

The priory was founded by Roesia de Verdun in 1239, and it was initially intended to house 14 Augustinian nuns and their prioress. De Verdun was buried at the priory in 1247, although during the dissolution of the monasteries some 300 years later her remains were exhumed and interred at nearby Belton Church. It is not known exactly how many occupants would have lived at the priory at any one time during its 300-year span as a religious house, but it appears to have been a thriving business community.

In 1536 the prioress, Agnes Litherland, received a licence

ABOVE The haunting ruins of the Grace Dieu Priory. It was one of the few Catholic establishments to be saved from the clutches of King Henry VIII's destructive reign.

from Henry VIII allowing the foundation to continue, despite the religious turmoil occurring at this point, and the convent was re-established 'in perpetuity'. However, just three years later the poor nuns were turned out, the prioress receiving a scant compensation of just 60 shillings.

One of the commissioners who dissolved the priory was John Beaumont of Thringstone, who took advantage of his position by buying Grace Dieu at his own valuation. He converted part of the priory into a residence, and although some of the ruins that stand today are medieval, they are primarily the remains of the Tudor home. In 1550 Beaumont became Master of the Rolls, and he again abused his position for personal gain. His misbehaviour at the Treasury was uncovered and his estates were surrendered to the King in 1552.

In 1553, Grace Dieu was granted to Francis, Earl of Huntingdon, though the widow of John Beaumont regained possession in 1574. It then passed to her son, Sir Francis Beaumont. The estate remained in the Beaumont family until 1690, when it was purchased by Sir Ambrose Phillips of Garendon, a wealthy Leicestershire landowner. His occupancy was brief, although not brief enough to prevent him from pulling down most of what remained of the priory church in 1696.

Grace Dieu Priory is renowned as one of the most haunted locations in Leicestershire. Since the 1920s, numerous people have claimed that they have witnessed ghosts in the vicinity of the ruins. Many accounts make reference to a woman in white, which may carry some significance, for although the priory at Grace Dieu was of the Augustinian Order, in which the nuns usually wear black habits, research in recent years has revealed that the sisters of Grace Dieu deviated from the norm and chose to wear white instead. Further research has uncovered the story of a monk who was in love with either a servant or another occupant of Grace Dieu. To end their relationship they were bricked into the walls at opposite sides of a room with only their eyes showing, so they could see each other, but not touch.

Hetty Wilson, from nearby Loughborough, described an incident that occurred when she was travelling home from nearby Coalville in 1926, where her father had been selling horses. She was just a child at the time and many years later Mrs Wilson described the events:

'We were passing the ruins when the horse driving our landau stopped. Its body was quivering. When we turned to see what was wrong, we saw six ghosts coming out of the nearby woods.'

Mrs Wilson remembered her father shouting 'Good God, ghosts!' and feeling terrified — in fact she was so scared that she hid her head from view.

'When I looked again, the ghosts had crossed the road and were heading up to the ruins. They wore white robes and had no faces or feet.'

The most famous sighting of all took place in 1954. On this occasion the driver of a bus heading for Shepshed pulled over at the lonely shelter opposite the ruins to pick up a woman in white. The bus door opened, but nobody boarded the vehicle. Both the driver and his conductor got off the bus to investigate, but were astonished to discover that the figure had simply vanished. This amazing story

Another event dates back to 1961, when 'the White Lady' was encountered by an off-duty policeman while walking his dog in the fields about half a mile away from the priory. He described his account as follows:

'On finishing duty, just before midnight on a warm April evening, I decided to take my boxer dog for a walk along the footpath across the fields opposite my home, where the Melrose Road housing estate now stands. It was a beautiful night, almost a full moon and not a cloud in the sky. We had been walking in the field for about 150 yards when suddenly my dog gave a deep-throated growl ... he continued to growl and came and stood closer to me, as if he was protecting me. I put my hand down to stroke him and the bristles along his back were stiff and rigid.

A few seconds after this there was a sudden chill in the air and a white form in the shape of a long cloak and hood glided by me and disappeared into a high hawthorn hedge about 25 yards from me. When this form went out of my sight, my dog quietened down and the chill went out of the air. The next day I told my neighbour of this and he said, "You have no doubt seen our local nun".'

BELOW *The ruined Great Hall of Grace Dieu Priory. In a state of collapse, the hall was too dangerous to venture into.*

turned the bus stop near the priory into a place of local legend — even today, over 50 years later, newspapers photograph the site to illustrate the eerie happenings at Grace Dieu Priory.

The story of the woman in white came to wider public attention in 1964, when Charlie Gough, who lived in the nearby village of Thringstone, described an experience he'd had some years earlier to a newspaper. He described the vision of a woman in white wearing a large, brimmed hat and recounted how, as he approached her for a closer look, she simply vanished.

Many people who have driven past Grace Dieu Priory have been startled by the fact they have driven straight through a lady standing in the middle of the road. In fact, the Haunted Britain team know of one person who swore she did this while on her way home one day.

The actual position of Grace Dieu Priory is also fascinating. It is believed to have been built on the end of a ley line, one of 32 such prehistoric alignments within Leicestershire and Rutland. During its time, Grace Dieu Priory may have been surrounded by large stones, with a ley line running through the centre of the site. Could this be an explanation for all the paranormal activity that has been witnessed in this area?

A HIKING WE WILL GO

The members of the Haunted Britain team arrived at Grace Dieu Priory at about 10:30pm on the night their investigation began and immediately headed to the fantastic ruins that lay before them. Many stories had circulated about Grace Dieu Priory over the years, but could they be proved — or even disproved — as the result of a thorough investigation?

Through a gate lay the historic landmark of Grace Dieu Priory. The main hall is still intact and the many other ruined walls signify a venue of great importance — and of a great size, with some rooms larger than a modern house. At the far end of the priory is the kitchen area, its magnificent fireplace and chimney still standing after over 700 years.

The team picked an area on the outside of the priory to set up a base, and lay their kit down to begin taking baseline tests. The moon was full that night, and the air had a quiet chill about it. However, nothing unusual was recorded or reported, and so the investigation began.

The obvious choice for the first location to investigate was the impressive main hall, which still stands at the heart of the priory. It was immediately noted that one window of the hall felt significantly colder than the rest when touched. Temperature readings were taken, and it was discovered that

RIGHT *The dead end of Grace Dieu Priory. No member of the Haunted Britain team liked the feeling here, and many light anomalies were captured.*

OPPOSITE *The great hall has played host to many different types of phenomena including temperature drops and full manifestations.*

the team was correct – this specific window was almost 8°C colder than any other area of the main hall. With no obvious explanation for this bizarre occurrence, the team began to ask questions and try and contact the spirit of 'the White Lady'.

During these attempts at communication, one team member held back and began to take photographs of the room.

'Got something!' he suddenly declared in an excited manner – and it was true, he had caught a strange yellow light on the wall of the main hall. Upon closer inspection the team discovered tiny reflective markers on the wall, which are used by restoration experts to check for movement and possible subsidence. However, under a torch or camera light these glowed white, not yellow. So what were the strange lights the team captured? No further explanation can be offered, but it should be noted that no cars passed by, nor were there any yellow lights near the team that night. The communication attempts continued for approximately half and hour, but the yellow lights did not appear again, nor could they be replicated by conventional means.

THE DEAD END

Next to the main hall is a strange corridor that ends without connecting to a room. Could this be the area where the two doomed lovers were bricked up? It is certainly possible, as there is only room for one or two people to fit inside the dead end of the corridor.

Almost immediately after the team arrived at this site, light anomalies began to emerge from the right-hand wall and disappear into the left-hand wall. At first it seemed as though they could be explained as dust or other airborne particles, however, they changed shape, direction and speed.

A common argument against paranormal orbs is that they can be explained away as dust. To become airborne, dust has to travel on a stream of air, which usually travels in one direction and at a constant and measurable speed. If a strange light appears during one of our investigations and changes direction or even changes shape – we do assume that it was caused by airborne particles, offering such anomalies up for further investigation. At Grace Dieu Priory a member of the team began to count the light anomalies as they emerged from the wall, quickly reaching 15 before stopping abruptly.

'Can you please do that again for us?' asked another team member who was holding a video camera.

And sure enough, three more light anomalies appeared on the right-hand wall and made their way gently towards the left, stopping often in midair and changing direction during their flight. The team were stunned, had they just witnessed a paranormal being reacting to a question? There was only way to make sure...

'Could you do that again, please?', the team member asked.

Two orbs appeared, moved through the space and disappeared into the left-hand wall. Again they seemed to meander along their path, stopping for brief moments as if to think about their destination, before continuing.

The team were shocked by the events that had just occurred; it seemed that these strange lights were appearing upon demand. So a further request was made ...

'We're sorry to keep asking, but could you do that again?' But no more light anomalies appeared.

The team began to analyse what had just occurred – never

ABOVE *A strange misty light was captured (on the left of the image). It was also captured by a camcorder from a different angle.*

before had they experienced so many light anomalies appear upon command. It really seemed as though somebody – or something – was trying to communicate with the members of the team. However, the critical point of view always remained, could it have been a coincidence? With no sign of further activity the Haunted Britain team continued their investigation into Grace Dieu Priory.

TOO MANY COOKS?

The team decided to venture into the ruins of the kitchen. The original room would have been large in size and the fireplace had obviously been much used over the years as there was smoke damage to the interior of the stone. The strangest sight in the kitchen was a very small wall, which runs diagonally across the room. There are no records to explain what this could have been and old engravings of the building do not appear to shed any light on the subject.

This section of Grace Dieu Priory was significantly colder than the rest of the site, and so baseline tests were taken again and recorded next to the original readings. By doing this,

the team had a constant set of measurements to work from.

After a short period of time, one member of the team pointed towards a rocky outcrop and described the strange feeling of being watched. He also described the figure of what looked like a small lady standing in front of a door. However, the area he was pointing to did not have a door, it was simply a ruin standing alone in the field. No amount of arguing could deter him from what he saw. The common assumption would be that the rocks had formed a recognizable shape and that this team member had simply picked up on it and was not able to shake the image from his mind.

Twenty minutes elapsed and the group decided to attempt to communicate with any spirits that may or may not be present.

'If there is anybody here, other than the team members, who wishes to talk with us, please feel free to do so – touch a team member, form a light or make a noise. We would like to know that somebody else still remains in the fantastic priory in which you lived.'

Suddenly, one of the group jumped, and stared in disbelief at the small wall that ran through the kitchen, in particular the plants that cascaded over it. The ferns seemed to have parted, despite the fact that there was no discernable wind that evening and no member of the team had walked through the plants to create the impression of movement.

With the remainder of the team now watching the wall, the plants moved back into their unified mass and a quick shine of the torch proved there were no animals close by that could have caused such a phenomenon.

With what seemed like a good deal of activity occurring at Grace Dieu Priory, the team decided to conduct a small séance to try and contact any spirits present. It is worth noting that the Haunted Britain team rarely conduct séances, but on this occasion it was agreed that such an event would be beneficial to the investigation. The team linked hands. Before the séance was initiated, the team took some time to bring psychic protection to the circle. It is often thought that by doing this you enter a state of readiness and also one of defence for yourself and the group involved. After ten minutes each team member was happy in what was about to occur and the séance began.

'IF THERE IS ANYBODY HERE ...'

As soon as the séance began, the team were startled to hear the sound of loud footsteps running around the group. The circle was closed and the group looked for a possible explanation. Every member of the team noted that the footsteps sounded as if they were coming from a hard surface, such as stone or concrete. The séance was conducted on soft ground, with only the small diagonal wall running alongside them.

Every member of the team heard this phenomenon, but none could replicate the noise they heard using any of the surrounding features, and all the individuals involved in the investigation were disturbed by what had just occurred. After a short period of time the team regained its composure and set about conducting a second séance to try and establish communication with the obvious presence that was alongside them.

Again psychic protection was taken, and the initial question was asked. This time it was followed by some frankly rather bizarre events...

Surrounding the séance was a series of three camcorders recording the scene from different angles to ensure that the evidence was satisfactory. As the séance continued, each one of these camcorders turned itself off. The batteries and tapes were new and all equipment was later checked to be fully functional, so how could this have happened? Was it just a technical glitch? If so, is it not an enormous coincidence that all three cameras turned off one after the other?

The air surrounding the team now became oppressive and the group no longer felt comfortable in their surroundings. With over 24 hours' worth of video footage captured they returned to base and began to view the evidence.

RIGHT *Lights from passing cars can play havoc with the equipment and could easily be misconstrued as strange lights.*

SUMMARY OF THE INVESTIGATION

The evidence captured by the Haunted Britain team at Grace Dieu Priory was quite incredible, with a flurry of orbs that appeared on command and photographic evidence of strange lights on flat surfaces that appeared from nowhere and disappeared very quickly. Some were not seen at the time and were only captured on digital equipment.

The glowing yellow lights that were caught on the wall of the Great Hall have left the team somewhat puzzled. The following things can be offered to explain the lights: a passing car, torchlight, a surveyors' sticker on the priory wall or a genuine paranormal event. At no point during the investigation of the main hall did a car pass the group on the road nearby. This can be verified by examining the video evidence and listening to the background noise – cars were recorded at different points during the investigation at the priory, and the sound was instantly recognizable as that of a vehicle passing by. However, this sound was *not* heard when the strange lights were captured.

The question of whether the strange lights were refraction from torches can be answered simply – none of the group carrying out the investigation that night carried torches that emitted a yellow beam. When the lights were initially captured, attempts were made to try and replicate them through conventional means. The surveyors' stickers on the side of the main hall emitted a bright white flare when a torch or digital camera was used their direction. The lights that were captured were yellow, and their flare did not match the proportions of the stickers. So then we come to the final explanation for the yellow lights – the paranormal.

Now we move on to the spectacular display of orbs that seemed to appear and disappear upon request. These light anomalies seem to fit into the category of dust or other airborne particles, with one notable exception – these strange lights appeared and disappeared on command. This is an amazing coincidence and it is possible that it was actually the air currents themselves that were being created when asked, as at no point did the team request further lights to appear, just for the event to happen again. This is one instance where the debate will continue for a lot longer.

With regards to the figure of a lady that was seen by a door, with nothing caught on video camera or by any other member of the team, we would have to file this under the category of personal experiences. Unfortunately, this is not quantifiable by conventional means, but still to this day the team member swears by what he saw.

One of the most fascinating incidents that took place during the investigation into Grace Dieu Priory was the apparent movement of the flora surrounding the kitchen. It was described by one team member as looking like somebody had just walked through the plants and had parted them with their stride – however no member of the group did this.

One of the only explanations we can offer for this strange incident would be that it was the result of animal movements. We noticed a lot of wildlife in the surrounding woodland, all of which seemed to disappear when our torches were cast across the trees. However, this is not evidence enough to discount the fact that an animal was brave enough to wander close to the team and cause the phenomenon that had occurred. Again this event will be a point of debate within the Haunted Britain team for many years to come.

And finally we come to our conclusions on the obvious phenomena that occurred during both attempts at a séance. First, there was the strange sound of footsteps that circled the team before disappearing. At no point was any member standing outside of the circle, as all cameras were operated remotely and each camera was filming a different angle of the scene, therefore offering a full 360° view. Upon watching the video evidence it is clear that nobody is seen walking around the group nor is there any wildlife that is wandering around the scene. This activity can only be assigned the title of 'paranormal', with no other explanation as to what occurred and with complete photographic footage of the event – we can offer no alternatives as to the origin of the sounds.

It is quite common for even the best equipment to fail when it is needed, which is why we always recommend taking spares. For three camcorders to fail within moments of each other is very rare, and, quite frankly, very bizarre. The camcorders were checked when the investigation concluded and all were found to be working perfectly, with no defective batteries, DVDs or other components. Due to the fact that we cannot be 100 per cent positive about the cause of this strange breakdown, we cannot dub what happened paranormal. However, we can add that since the investigation into Grace Dieu Priory, our camcorders have only ever failed once.

Grace Dieu Priory is a brilliant location for investigation, steeped in ghostly history and featuring some striking architecture that easily depicts the majesty of the site. The stories emanating from the priory still echo round Leicestershire, and the Haunted Britain team have a feeling that they always will.

PLEASLEY VALE MILLS
OUTGANG LANE, MANSFIELD, NOTTINGHAMSHIRE, NG19 8RL

PREVIOUS SIGHTINGS AND EXPERIENCES

- The sounds of trolley carts being pushed along
- Unexplained feelings of depression
- The sounds of young children playing in the woods
- The apparition of a man who is claimed to have been murdered in the lake nearby
- The apparition of a lady named Annie, who is said to have murdered somebody
- The infamous haunted toilets .... and more!

THE LOCATION AND ITS HISTORY

Surrounded by ancient woodland and steeped in history, local legends and folklore, Pleasley Vale Mills in Nottinghamshire is a site renowned for its haunting atmosphere. Many people have seen and heard inexplicable things here, and the Haunted Britain team was invited to investigate this famous factory by Rupert Mole, a company that now inhabits part of the location.

It was one William Hollins who decided, along with four

ABOVE *Pleasley Vale Mills is a spectacular location with an abundance of paranormal sightings and experiences, witnessed by many visitors over the years. Drenched in history, it is one of the country's most haunted places.*

other respected businessmen, that Pleasley Vale would be a good place to construct a cotton mill. The textile industry was in its infancy at this point, but the partnership knew that it was about to grow. The vale was rich in resources — stone, timber and water — and the river nearby had already been dammed. There was a water wheel in place, which was used to drive the bellows and steam hammer. The area also had its own microclimate, which provided the constant humidity required to spin the cotton.

In 1786 the grounds were excavated by an archaeologist named Hayman Rooke, and Roman coins were found at Stuffyn Wood Farm, which belonged to the Pleasley estate. During the development of a garage to the rear of Pleasley house in 1962, a cave was exposed. Inside this space the bones of a woolly rhinoceros, a mammoth and evidence of a prehistoric tribe were discovered. The remains of a Viking settlement have also been discovered at nearby Mansfield.

Many people who once worked at the mills have come back to visit the site since, and Rupert Mole have pieced together a profile of the fair but firm working conditions that were present under William Hollins' employment. He built a village store, a school, a mechanics institute, a reform church and a bathhouse for the employees of the cotton mills.

The company that operated the mill closed in 1987 and the buildings fell into decline. Bolsover District Council declared the vale a conservation area and now owns the site, which is home to many thriving businesses. There is certainly a rich and strong vein of history at Pleasley Vale Mills, and it seems there is much more to discover. Previous guests at the location have witnessed some striking phenomena, so it was with a certain degree of apprehension that the Haunted Britain team entered Mill One, and began to conduct their investigation.

THE INVESTIGATION BEGINS

Missing out on a magnificent buffet spread laid on for visitors to the mills, the team was eager to get going – no time for food, it wastes valuable minutes. Making its way outside, the group set off down the driveway, passing alongside the old Governor's mansion. Set high up in the woods, this large, dilapidated Victorian house is spooky enough during daylight hours and it proved even more ominous at night. Partially hidden by a surrounding wall, the ruined remains of this once impressive dwelling stare down at passers-by through a few overgrown trees.

Numerous accounts have described the sight of a woman dressed in white who simply stands and stares out of an upstairs window, and some people have observed the same apparition on a balcony at the front of the building. Although the team would have liked to get inside the old house, unfortunately the driveway was the closest that it could reach, as the property has been declared unsafe due to structural problems. This was a real shame, as the team was convinced that there could be some truth behind the sightings that have been reported.

The woods that the team were going to be investigating were at the back of the mills. This meant a walk round the man-made lake that stood to the side of Mill One. Also supposedly haunted, the lake was commissioned by the Governor who inhabited the house, as

he was not overly keen on the view from his front window. To add character, he created the lake with a small island in the centre. This also helped to run the mill as the water was used to power the vast amount of machinery inside the factory.

The lake is the site of a haunting that is believed to be the spirit of a young man who committed suicide, possibly as a result of unrequited love. However, there has been much speculation, particularly from members of this unfortunate man's family, that the cause of his death was somewhat more sinister. Circumstances surrounding this individual's end have always been suspicious and many believe that he was in fact the victim of foul play. However, a verdict of suicide was determined and without further evidence, which is highly unlikely, this will remain the official outcome. But the man's ghost is said to roam the lake and parts of the mill. Many say he returns to seek justice for his untimely death, others simply believe that his fate has left him in limbo, forever stuck between the living and the dead.

Although the team didn't spend any time investigating the area around the lake it definitely felt very creepy. This feeling may have had something to do with the surrounding woods, which are very dark and enclosed; it may also have been the result of the soaring chimney and many windows of the mill buildings, which loomed over the team. Without any detailed

RIGHT *Many people have witnessed spirits or ghosts moving around the Mill in all the locations.*

LEFT *The area near the toilets is one of the most active locations, one team member was brave enough to stay there alone for the night.*

accounts of the exact activity that had taken place and no precise location of the spot where it had been witnessed, it was too big an area to investigate. So the team moved on to the woods.

IS ANYBODY THERE?

The strange thing about Pleasley Vale Mills is that they are completely concealed from civilization. With the exception of the chimney, none of the huge mill buildings are visible from the main roads and the wooded valley helps to seclude this location from the rest of the world.

Bathed in moonlight, the woods at the rear of the building have frequently been described as one of the most haunted locations at the site. Child-like voices, whispering and playful activity have been witnessed during many of the investigations that have taken place. One area of the woods where a lot activity has been reported is beneath the old railway bridge.

The team made its way across a small field towards the large arched construction. It was obvious that it had been used as a den by a group of teenagers, as there was evidence of recent rubbish and debris. However, it seemed that the team wouldn't be disturbed during their investigation.

With an abundance of wildlife and the moonlight casting an array of shadows on the scene, it was difficult to gauge what could be deemed paranormal. Great attention was taken to keep movement and noise to a minimum, because the acoustics in the tunnel made everything sound much louder, and locating the source of sounds was particularly difficult. Luckily, it was a relatively still night with hardly any wind to take into account. This meant that any movement of branches or objects would have to be made by something actually moving them.

A dictaphone was placed on the equipment case in the centre of the tunnel. With the tapes running, the team began to ask any spirits present to try and make contact with them. There was a large amount of moisture in the air and it was humid, so any photographs taken would inevitably capture a lot of mist and airborne water particles that could easily be mistaken as orbs. This had to be considered when reviewing any images taken.

Unfortunately, after about 15 minutes it appeared that nothing was going to happen at this site. A few anomalous noises were heard, but these could be discounted as movements made by small animals. However, just as the group was leaving the tunnel, one team member noted that the air temperature suddenly dropped – it changed from being relatively cool to icy cold. This was quantified by the digital thermometer, which showed a drop of over 2°C. This is an unusual occurrence in the space of just a few minutes, but add to this the fact that the area was under cover and it became extraordinary. Was someone making his or her presence known, or was it a natural drop in temperature? Without more equipment and more time this was almost impossible to determine, but what *was* certain was that things didn't feel right.

PLAYING HIDE AND SEEK

Time was running out, so the team members decided to move on to another part of the woods. They were led through a small opening in the trees to a narrow winding footpath. Once again, it was difficult to determine if any of the sounds and rustling noises that were heard along the way were paranormal or just the wildlife shuffling around.

The team stopped at an opening where the path split into two, where it was advised that many people had heard the sound of young children playing in this part of the woods. The trees created many shadows and it was easy for the team to mistake shapes and movement of branches as something more than natural. However, there was a genuine feeling that perhaps the group was not alone and some of the movement along one of the paths may well have been created by something that was more likely to be paranormal than normal.

One of the members of the team took this opportunity to venture further into the woods and investigate some strange noises. As he reached a corner he began to call out, asking any spirit present to make itself known. Suddenly, one of the other team members felt a strong and forceful draught behind his legs. Nobody else witnessed this, but they could also clarify that there were no sudden gusts of wind to cause such a strange sensation.

The same individual then described the feeling that someone was standing behind him. If this area was haunted by the spirits of young children, could they have been playing with the team? Were they playing hide and seek? If they were, they were extremely good at hiding! The individual still had the sensation that someone was there, but whoever it was seemed very reluctant to let themselves be seen or heard.

The group carried on trying to establish contact with any spirits present. There was still the suspicion that the group was not completely alone, but whoever was with the team wanted to keep themselves well hidden. At this point, some strange noises were heard in the area towards the path leading to the mills. Attempting to keep calm and maintain an open-minded approach, the team kept its cool. A noise that sounded like the booming bass of a car stereo was heard, accompanied by the sound of young voices. Concerned that they were about to be interrupted, the group began to make its way back to the mills. Time was moving on and there was plenty more to see inside Pleasley Mills.

There was no doubt that the woods were exceedingly creepy, but then again, which woods aren't in the middle of the night? Whether or not these woods are haunted is not something that could be determined completely from the small amount of time that the team spent there — but that isn't to say that they aren't revisited by former residents of

RIGHT *Pleasley Vale Mills embodies a dark and foreboding piece of history. With the exception of the chimney, none of the huge mill buildings are visible from the main roads and the wooded valley helps to seclude this location from the rest of the world. The woods at the rear of the building have frequently been described as one of the most haunted locations at the site.*

the mill and the surrounding villages who've since passed on. However, these spirits certainly didn't feel like making themselves known on this occasion.

WHERE'S BILLY?

The second location for the team to investigate was the top floor inside the mill. Unfortunately, due to the unsafe nature of the floor, all that was accessible was a very gloomy and dishevelled stairwell and landing. An uninviting door stood between the team and the mill's mysterious fourth floor with its abundance of secrets.

According to many psychics and sensitive visitors to Pleasley Mills, this area is one of the homes of a notorious individual by the name of Billy. This rather unsavoury character, described as an evil and despicable man, was apparently responsible for tormenting, and possibly even murdering, many female workers at the mill. One day, however, his reign of terror was dramatically brought to an end. Billy was sup-

BELOW *The stairs to the upper room. Many light anomalies were captured seemingly walking up the stairs in a strange form of motion. One orb in particular looked as though it was actually moving up the staircase towards the team – travelling not quickly or randomly, but very slowly and methodically.*

posedly lured to his death by one of the more provocative female staff members. More than likely very proud of his infamous antics, Billy has become as feared after his death as he was in his short life.

He has made himself known to a wealth of visitors and investigators, in particular those of the female persuasion. It was hoped that the presence of women during this investigation would spark his enthusiasm and that Billy would make his presence known.

Everyone assembled in the tight confines of the small room and along the stairs. Taking up their positions, they began by standing quietly and adjusting themselves to their surroundings. There was no heating or insulation of any kind in the vicinity and the air temperature was relatively cool. With more people in the room it was expected that the temperature would rise very gradually as a result of the body heat that was generated. One member of the team was positioned at the top of the staircase and pointed the video camera down to the bottom of the stairs where another member had taken up position.

To avoid stirring up any dust, everyone present was asked to keep movement to a minimum and to take into account the fact that many images might be affected by dust particles. However, this did not mean that light anomalies would not occur, but it was going to be more difficult to distinguish between dust and actual paranormal occurrences.

COME AND JOIN US

With everyone settled, the team began to film the scene. Within only a few minutes the camera at the top of the stairs began to pick up strange light anomalies. What distinguished these orbs from dust particles was the clarity and pattern of movement involved. What started as a few sporadic lights traversing the scene was enhanced, as the lights appeared to increase in size and clarity. These anomalies appeared to have a distinct purpose in their direction of movement, unlike dust, which moves in a more random manner. One orb in particular looked as though it was actually moving up the staircase towards the team – travelling not quickly or randomly, but very slowly and methodically. Could this signal somebody coming to join the group?

Then the light anomalies stopped ascending the dark staircase. Something caused one member of the team to focus her attentions on the door on the opposite side of the landing. She turned the camera she was holding to face the locked door and asked for anyone present to make themselves known to the team. She then specifically asked Billy to come forward if he was in the room with them – it didn't take long

ABOVE *The upper room plays host to a number of ghosts or spirits. Many of those present described a sense of being watched and felt uncomfortable and uneasy.*

to get a response. Almost instantly, the light anomalies that had been on the stairs appeared to change their location.

Once again, unlike dust, these light anomalies were slow and performed precise movements. One orb in particular loomed extremely brightly and looked as though it had come from the door towards the camera, it then encircled another female member of the team who was standing in the room. As this happened the woman exclaimed that she suddenly felt extremely cold – at this point she knew nothing about the light anomaly that had just passed in front of her. The light remained around for a matter of seconds and then promptly disappeared. Had this been some type of insect – and none had been reported by anyone present – it would not simply disappear when it moved in front of the camera. The fact that the strange light and the drop in temperature felt by the woman coincided in this manner only gave more credence to the possibility that the two things were linked and therefore more likely to be attributed to the paranormal.

To back up the woman's claim, a temperature reading was taken of everyone in the room. The majority of those present had a body temperature of between 24–25°C, however, quite significantly, the woman who had experienced the peculiar sense of suddenly feeling very cold had a body temperature of just 20°C – a full 5 degrees lower than the average temperature of her colleagues. She was also colder than the room temperature. Was this mere coincidence or paranormal? The very correlation between the two events was hugely fascinating in itself, but the evidence that supported these occurrences clearly made these findings more substantial.

Intrigued by what had happened, the team asked the woman to move away from the area in which she was standing and appealed for someone else to take her place in the area in which she had witnessed this cold spot. As soon as she moved the feeling of cold seemed to disappear. Another team member then took up the same position and agreed that there was definitely a drop in temperature from where she had been standing previously. The team member who had initially been standing in the cold spot began to feel warmer again and a temperature reading taken just a few moments later confirmed that her body had returned to a normal, comfortable body temperature.

Unfortunately, the light anomalies and temperature changes were the only incidents that took place in this somewhat feared and avoided area, and although these events

provided some excitement for the team, they were no closer to confirming whose spirit lurks in the shadows of this menacing corner of Pleasley Mills. Many of those present described a sense of being watched and felt uncomfortable and uneasy. Could this have been Billy suppressing his intimidating antics? Or was it the ghost of one of those poor souls who lost their life at his hands or within the confines of the mill? Without further evidence, it would be difficult to make a firm judgement.

AN ABUNDANCE OF ORBS

You would expect that once you had seen one orb you had seen them all, but nothing could have prepared the team for what they were about to experience.

ABOVE *The old Governor's mansion near to Pleasley Vale Mills is also said to be haunted. This large, dilapidated Victorian house is in ruins and the property has been declared unsafe due to structural problems. There have been several sightings of a woman, dressed in white, who stands staring out of the upstairs window or appears on the balcony.*

The final location that the team was to investigate was an office, which, according to previous visitors and investigators, was one of the most paranormally active areas at the site. Since the conversion of the mills into business premises, it has become difficult to distinguish exactly which parts of the mills were used for what purpose. This office could have had any number of uses within the day-to-day workings of a busy cotton factory.

Reasonably modern in appearance, this was not your habitual haunted setting. The room is modern and completely void of furnishings of any kind. As atmospheres go, it was bland and unimpressive, but something was definitely hanging in the air. It was a feeing that nobody could really explain, but it was certainly not welcoming or inviting.

The moment one member of the team entered the room she felt apprehensive, and all the hairs on the back of her neck stood on end. For some reason, she also began to feel very nauseous and a little unwell. The team members took their places around the edge of the room and started the cameras rolling. They didn't have to wait long, as the room seemed to attract a plethora of light anomalies almost instantly.

At first, the lights appeared very slowly and intermittently and there was nothing to get particularly excited about. As the vigil continued, the light anomalies began to get brighter, more definite and more frequent. The pattern of movement changed from relatively random to a specific course – these strange, travelling lights seemed to have a positive and clear direction. It is extremely unusual for a dust particle to have such a purposeful route.

If these anomalies had been insects, somebody on the team would have noticed their presence, as it was a very confined space. However, at this point the team was still worried that the lights could be explained as dust or other airborne particles. However, the team's view of its findings soon changed as two of the group started to pick up the same light anomalies on two separate cameras that were set at different angles.

The way that dust particles reflect light means that it would be very unusual – in fact almost impossible – for two cameras placed at different locations to pick up the same miniscule speck of dust. The team were more than intrigued, but concealed their excitement and remained calm.

The orbs just kept coming. They were irregular and infrequent and appeared to stop at one point, but then they began to pursue the same erratic behaviour. Being professional investigators, the Haunted Britain team members refused to be drawn into the subjective train of thought that everything without an immediate explanation must be paranormal and they were careful to constantly examine the possibilities of how all this light activity could be explained. Nevertheless, it was proving difficult to pass this off as a completely natural occurrence. Other people in the room had video cameras, but they weren't capturing the same phenomena, so what – or who – was causing this abundance of strange lights and flashes.

Then something extremely strange began to occur – the orbs started to change into longer streaks of light, resembling spheres with long wispy trails. These changes were noticed not on just one camera, but both cameras being used by the team. It was becoming increasingly difficult to give any reasonable explanation for these anomalies.

One team member decided to move position, shifting to a location within the room where they felt the most activity. Others also decided to move, but some stayed where they were, especially those that were getting such interesting results. The team settled in their new positions. Two members had moved to sit near the large double doors that led to the corridor, one of them had felt a strange sensation as they stepped through the doors, so it seemed an appropriate place to return to.

The camera carried on rolling and dictaphones constantly recorded the sound in the room, in the hope that EVP would be captured. There were still a few orbs moving from the centre of the room towards the member of the team who had reported the activity, and both cameras were picking up the same light anomalies. For some reason, the area that one of them had chosen to sit in began to make her feel nauseous and she started to get more and more uncomfortable.

A few minutes passed, then several members of the team heard a strange noise coming from the corridor, as if something was being dragged or scraped along the floor. One of them jumped up immediately to investigate. There was nobody around and everyone else present in the building was too far away from the group to cause any sort of disturbance in this area. Leaving their positions within the office, two team members moved into the corridor to see if any more activity was going to occur.

Back in the room a few people sensed the presence of children and also felt as if they were being watched. It wasn't a particularly unpleasant feeling, and nobody felt unusually anxious or afraid. The atmosphere was relatively calm, and despite the amount of light anomalies that were picked up, there was very little else to support the belief that anything significant was going to occur. The team were careful to stay as still as possible, which meant that it was difficult to detect cold spots or warm spots, as this would disturb too much dust and noise.

Noises in the corridor

Something a little more unusual was happening in the corridor. Both investigators had heard the sounds of footsteps coming from a floor above – which would have been completely normal if there was a floor above them for someone to walk along! The level above had been completely demolished when it was declared unsafe. There was only one entrance point on to the roof and that was via the door near the staircase, which was securely locked – there was no possible way that any one could gain access.

It was certainly something worthy of the paranormal and both of the individuals present had witnessed the same noise. One of them had also described hearing the sound of squeaking and whirring, much like wheels or machinery. It was only when the group reconvened that another member of the team revealed that this sound had been heard before. It was believed to be the sound of a tea trolley rolling along the corridor and it had been heard on many occasions by workers at the mill and various mediums and paranormal investigators.

Neither person knew the history of the building or had any knowledge of any of the previous sightings, so the noises could not have been the result of suggestion. For the same noise to be heard by two unsuspecting people only gave more credence to the phenomena that had been witnessed.

When the team listened to the dictaphone tapes later that evening, a strange disembodied noise was heard above the voices of the two individuals stationed in the corridor. After a thorough analytical process, it was determined that this noise was not created by either of the individuals in the room at the time nor was it created by anybody else in the immediate vicinity. The noise sounded very much like a child crying or shouting out and there were certainly no children present in the building at the time. Coupled with the fact that some of the investigators had described the feeling of children around them, this seemed to be a very credible paranormal experience.

Many children would have lost their lives at the mill as a result of illness and injuries caused by the heavy and powerful machinery, so it is definitely possible that this location is haunted by the spirits of the poor boys and girls whose lives were cut short.

Out of time

Unfortunately, time had caught up with the group and the vigils came to an end. The two groups joined back up and headed back through the maze of corridors to the meeting room for breakfast and a quick get together.

The dictaphone was kept running as the team made their way back. All the way along they were discussing what they had heard and, despite feeling very tired, the mood and atmosphere remained high and cheerful. Nobody appeared to be apprehensive or displaying any behaviour that would usually accompany individuals consumed by fear! All in all, everyone felt very comfortable.

Summary of the investigation

Pleasley Vale Mills is a spectacular location with an abundance of paranormal sightings and experiences witnessed by many visitors over the years. Drenched in a history that includes murderous villains, terrible suffering and a suspicious suicide, it is bound to be crawling with rumours that make it one of the country's most haunted places.

With so many areas to investigate, the Haunted Britain team found itself stretched and would ideally want to perform more investigations and experiments than they were able to complete on this occasion. There was certainly *something* in the atmosphere at Pleasley Mills and the site has everything that a haunted property needs – a colourful life, a wealth of strong characters, a fair share of tragedy and a spooky skyline that adds to the air of suspense and trepidation.

So is Pleasley Vale Mill haunted? It certainly seems to be and from the previous stories of ghostly encounters that many paranormal groups have reported, it is a definite possibility. With more equipment, experiments and especially time, the Haunted Britain team are positive that they would find more evidence to support these claims. Why not go along and see for yourself? You may find what we were looking for without even trying!

However, when examining the evidence recorded on tape a strange breathing noise was heard as they neared the stairwell that the infamous Billy was known to frequent. The tone and gruffness of the breath indicated that the noise was definitely made by a man and it was extremely close to the recording equipment. It wasn't heard by any of the team as they were exiting the area and nobody except the person holding the equipment was close enough to the dictaphone to make such a noise. This person was discounted as the noise wasn't in the same tone as his voice.

Was Billy trying to make his presence known again? Or was it another spirit attempting to make contact? Unfortunately, the team will probably never know unless they get the opportunity to investigate this huge location again, what was clear was that the group was not alone and there was plenty more to discover. If only they had more time.

ABOVE *Although the look of the corridor is modern, it is said to be one of the most haunted sections of the mill. One of the team members described hearing the sound of squeaking and whirring, much like wheels or machinery. It was only when the group reconvened that another member of the team revealed that this sound had been heard before. It was believed to be the sound of a tea trolley rolling along the corridor and it had been heard on many occasions by workers at the mill and various mediums and paranormal investigators.*

THE ROYAL VICTORIA PATRIOTIC BUILDING
FITZHUGH GROVE, TRINITY ROAD, LONDON, SW18 3SX

PREVIOUS SIGHTINGS AND EXPERIENCES

- Soldiers seen in the courtyards and various rooms
- Clinical smells
- The smell of burning in the main tower
- The sound of a young girl crying and screaming
- Cold spots
- Disembodied footsteps and sounds of movement
- Anomalous sounds, bangs and voices

THE LOCATION

Set on the edge of Wandsworth Common, amongst modern blocks of flats stands the magnificent, palatial Royal Victoria Patriotic Building. Built in 1857, the shadowy gothic towers, ornate stone carvings and elegant Victorian architecture could be mistaken for a building with much more prestige and importance than its original purpose.

There is no doubt that this amazing and extravagant building looks more like a palace. Nevertheless, the outside is far more opulent than its interior. The imposing front doors stand at the base of the central tower above which is a large detailed sculpture depicting George and the Dragon, signifying strength and triumph.

Speaking of towers, this building has plenty. Well hidden from the bustling traffic, the building is barely visible from the road except for the towers that protrude above the tree tops. In daylight they might be described as romantic but once darkness descends they create a chilling and menacing skyline that would befit any creepy horror film.

Inside is a maze of rooms, corridors and courtyards, together with a coach house and chapel. The interior decoration is plain and somewhat featureless with the exception of a few gothic finials on banisters and decorative cornices and archways. It still resembled a school or formal establishment. On the other hand, thinking about its history, this wasn't that surprising, but from the beautiful and lavish exterior it was certainly unexpected.

In the 1950s it was sold to the council to use as a school but soon it fell into a state of disrepair. It was put up for sale in the 1980s but its £4million price tag along with the amount of restoration required put many developers off. Eventually, a local entrepreneur convinced the Greater London Council to sell it to him for the measly sum of £1.00, with the stipulation that they must use their own funds to restore it to its former glory. The project took six years, but the conversion has certainly brought this amazing structure back to life.

Now, this impressive former orphanage, hospital, prison and school has been remodelled into 27 stylish, contemporary and luxurious apartments that are home to some of London's affluent professionals including artists, architects and not to mention a few famous musicians. Other areas have been turned into offices, studios, a drama and music school and the aptly named La Gothique French restaurant.

THE HISTORY

The Crimean War in the 19th century created an abundance of widows. Many servicemen were killed in battle and as a result Prince Albert chaired the Patriotic Fund which collected money for the injured service men and their dependents who were deemed in need of assistance. The wealth of public feeling, sympathy and patriotism provided the Royal Commission with well over £1.5million to help, enough money to dedicate an entire building to the worthy cause. They began constructing an asylum for 300 orphaned daughters of those who gave their lives for their country.

A plot of land on Wandsworth Common was sold to the Royal Commision by the Lord Of The Manor – the Earl Of Spencer. Queen Victoria laid the first stone in a prestigious ground-breaking ceremony on 11th July 1857 and it was completed within two years. The asylum accepted its first residents on the 1st July 1859 and 150 girls made the building their home. Full capacity wasn't reached until a few years later when an infirmary was added.

The 'inmates' of the asylum were initially taught in domestic service, and conventional schooling took second place until the curriculum demanded more formal education. The large building was difficult to keep and expensive to staff. So the teaching of domestic service skills proved to be extremely useful as the residents provided the majority of the manual labour required.

It was far from a life of luxury and easy living. The treatment of the orphans was near to diabolical. Hygiene dictated that the girls were made to stand naked in the courtyard to be hosed down, and their heads were shaved to avoid head lice. It was a meagre existence for these poor unfortunates, but it beat being on the streets. Life was hard for them and they had to endure many long winter nights without heating or any fire for warmth. Those who complained would have found themselves in severe trouble with the Matron and punishments were harsh.

Unfortunately, the strictness and unapproachable attitude displayed by the teaching staff had its flaws and subsequently led to the death of one of the young orphans. In January 1862, Charlotte Jane Bennett was locked in solitary confinement in the Superintendent's bathroom for insubordination. The consequences for the young lady were disastrous. A fire broke out in the tower where she was being

OPPOSITE Set on the edge of Wandsworth Common, and built in 1857, the magnificent, gothic Royal Victoria Patriotic Building has had many uses. The former orphange, hospital, prison and school has recently been remodelled into 27 stylish, contemporary and luxurious apartments.

RIGHT A terrible fire ripped through the RVPB in 1981, and one of the victims is said to still walk the building to this day.

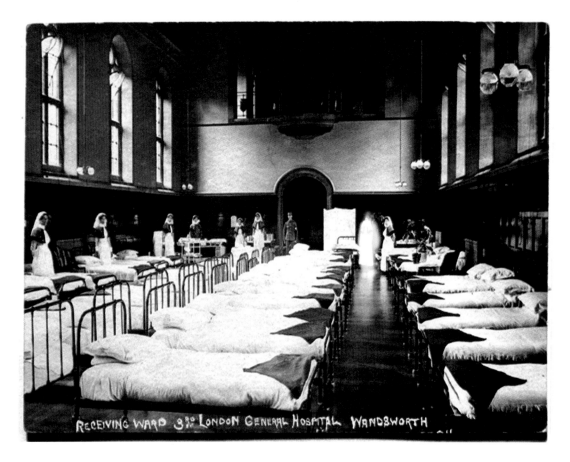

RECEIVING WARD 3RD LONDON GENERAL HOSPITAL WANDSWORTH

Aʙᴏᴠᴇ *The receiving ward at the RVPB, which was the 3rd London General Hospital during the First World War. Thousands of servicemen were treated here, many of whom died from their injuries. During the Second World War the building was used to interrogate prisoners, a far more sinister purpose.*

There were thousands of casualties and eventually they were forced to overspill into small outbuildings erected to relieve overcrowding and avoid the spreading of disease and infection. Gradually the number of patients rose to 1800. Although the majority of the injured would have made a full recovery and went on to rehabilitation, many would have died from their injuries. This could explain some of the activity and phenomena witnessed at the hall.

The Great War ended and the orphans returned to their exquisite home. It was a brief stay however as they were once more evacuated in 1938 at the beginning of the Second World War. This time they were all sent to a school in Hertfordshire and they never returned to the Royal Victoria Patriotic Asylum. They remained at their new home until the orphanage was closed in 1972, not through a lack of funding but more pleasantly a lack of orphans.

held on the second day of her confinement. Hearing her screams the other children were too scared to alert any of their stern teachers. She burnt to death. She is now believed to be one of the most prevalent ghosts in the building and can often be heard crying and screaming from the tower.

The orphanage was nearly closed down with the scandal of an orphan in the government's care dying such a horrific death. This, along with allegations of terrible living conditions, almost put an end to the asylum, but a radical shake-up allowed the charity to carry on its much needed work, but under much closer supervision.

In 1914, whilst the children were away on their summer holidays, the orphanage was taken over by the Government when war was declared in Europe. Upon their return the children of the asylum were moved into local houses. The building became a military hospital and wounded servicemen were brought in to the hospital from the coast by any means of transport possible and with the main Wandsworth train line running along the outskirts of the building, it made easy access for the patients.

A more sinister use became the building's new purpose during the Second World War, when it was used by MI6 and MI5 as a detention centre. Prisoners of War were held there and interrogated. It is also believed that two of the courtyards were used as a firing range for carrying out death sentences. Many people have felt unnatural chills in these areas but so far there has been very little evidence to support these claims.

One very important 'guest' was held at His Majesty's Pleasure in the cells that now make up a wine cellar owned by La Gothique restaurant. Rudolph Hess was captured after parachuting in to Scotland on a 'peace keeping' mission. He was quickly detained and interrogated at the Royal Victoria Patriotic Building, before being moved to a more secure location for imprisonment.

He was then taken back to Germany to stand trial at Nuremburg. Despite being less than completely sane, he was found guilty and sentenced to life imprisonment. He committed suicide in 1987 at the age of 92, the last surviving henchman of Adolf Hitler.

After the war the building was once again used for education, but this time it became a teacher-training college and then a school. The upkeep of the building appeared too much for the school to cope with and it fell into disrepair. The school closed in the 1970s and the building was left empty. Unfortunately it was the victim of vandalism and was close to being demolished until it was saved by protests from local conservation groups. The building was awarded a Grade II Listing but it proved difficult to sell due to the extent of restoration required.

Eventually it was bought by a development company and restored to its former glory and into the building you see today. There is definitely an air of mystery and intrigue surrounding this fantastic location and the team couldn't wait to get inside.

THE INVESTIGATION BEGINS

The team pulled up to the location, and immediately were in awe of the unbelievably outstanding architecture. The blocks of 1970s flats lining the driveway gave way to reveal this bizarre and eccentric gothic masterpiece. They entered the cobbled courtyard which contained the original coach house

BELOW *The entrance to the garden — many different feelings were reported here from oppression to relaxation and fear.*

and stables. That evening the restaurant was being used for a wedding so there was quite a lot of ambient noise and music blaring out from the disco, but with such a large premises to conduct the investigation in, the team were not too perturbed.

They met their contact, who was the owner of one of the apartments within the building. Entering his flat the team were astounded at the contrast between past and present. From the very historic and old exterior to this modern, clean and contemporary style dwelling. It had minimalism down to a fine art.

The owner was a friend of one of Haunted Britain's team members and she had been invited previously to the location to perform a small investigation as he had experienced some strange occurrences in his flat. On her first visit she communicated with the spirit of a young soldier by the name of Tommy. It was believed that he had unfortunately died at the building when it was used as a hospital during the war.

Being a sensitive she helped this poor young man find his way and also managed to reunite him with his mother. After a quick drink the team were ready to start the tour of the building. As they were exiting the apartment, she stopped and turned to her husband.

'Tommy was here again,' she said with a smile on her face. 'He came to thank me for helping him.' She was clearly very happy that she had made contact and managed to help this poor young man.

ABOVE *During its past, the RVPB has played host to the forces, including MI5, MI6 and MI9. Prisoners of War were held there and interrogated and it is believed that two of the courtyards were used as a firing range for carrying out death sentences. Many people have felt unnatural chills in these areas.*

The rest of the team hadn't been given much information about what she had found on her first visit. All they knew was that her mini investigation had revealed some interesting paranormal phenomena and she had requested that the whole team should be allowed to conduct a larger and more in-depth study. With the agreement of some of the other residents the team were allowed into the main communal areas as well as a couple of the private apartments and offices.

Their first port of call was the main entrance hall. The tour led them around the outside of the building down a dark driveway. The main gates to the side of the building were just visible as the sky started to darken. The thin, fenced-in pathway then opened into a car park, bordered by a small fence and tall trees. This was the first time the rest of the team had seen the front of the building.

Impressive yet imposing, the soaring towers that made this building so striking from a distance were now clearly visible.

Despite all the modern surroundings it was easy to imagine how it would have looked when it was first built and one member of the team had a mental picture of young children in crisp, white pinafore dresses lining up outside the doors ready to go inside. It wasn't until later in the evening when the team were given access to some of the old photographs that it was realised that her vision was more than just her imagination.

An early engraving of the girls dining at the orphanage showed them in the same white overalls and another depicted them in the 'Royal Victoria Patriotic Crocodile', a very long line of the girls walking in procession through the common. She hadn't seen these pictures before but the images that she had were so similar that the team couldn't help but think that this was an unbelievable coincidence.

THE ENTRANCE HALL

Once inside, the team were confused. What looked like such a regal and extraordinary gothic wonder from the outside suddenly became a little less impressive and more ordinary. The hall was big and empty. Three archways led through into the main staircases of the central tower and began the maze of corridors and stairwells. It was obvious that more interest had been taken in getting the apartments and private areas up to a luxurious standard, whilst the public areas and entrances were just given a coat of paint and a good clean. This is not to say that it was sub-standard in any way, far from it, but the contrast was visible.

The tour took them through into the Pond Courtyard, appropriately named after the large stone pond in the shape of a cross in the centre. It seemed relatively calm and peaceful but there was also something that gave some of the team an uneasy feeling. It was easy to feel a little daunted as the courtyard was overlooked by many windows from residents' flats and walkways around its perimeter. However, one particular door seemed to disturb two members of the team more than anywhere else.

Both members felt like they were being watched from behind the glass panel in the door and they couldn't help but feel a little on edge. Although nothing was caught on camera there was an interesting phenomena caught on a dictaphone. The sounds of footsteps in the corridor that could not be heard at the time of the investigation were faintly heard striding through the part near the door where the members felt particularly uncomfortable.

BAD VIBES IN THE BEDROOM

Time was limited at this location and it was important to get around as many places as possible in the short space of time we had been allocated. A quick phone call was made to the owner of one of the flats that the team had gained access to. This particular private residence was at the top of a flight of stairs that spiralled its way up into the south tower.

The owner hadn't encountered anything specifically paranormal in the flat, but admitted that he had experienced some strange occurrences and, given the history of the building, believed that it could be a possibility. He agreed to let the team conduct a vigil in his home.

As this was a private location the team were very careful not encourage anything into the flat that might cause bad feeling or unwanted activity, so they chose not to include any of the more provocative techniques in their vigil in this room. The owner felt that if anywhere, the most active place would be the bedroom, and so with his permission the team made there way up to the bedroom area.

It was split into two levels. A dressing room occupied the lower part of the room with a laddered staircase that led to the sleeping area. This area was clearly an addition to the original structure due to the fact that the floor level sat half way up one of the windows creating a lovely low level window. The room stretched up into the eaves of the tower with beautiful high vaulted ceilings. It was hard to imagine that this was anything like a school, hospital or even a prison. Such modern decoration and such clean, crisp structured design was a definite contrast with the Victorian gothic setting. But that's not to say that modern surroundings mean no ghosts... far from it!

At first the team felt nothing in particular but as the vigil went on they noticed that the air was feeling very heavy. Although the room was light and airy it began to feel quite claustrophobic. Two members sat by

the top of the staircase. The team was initially very comfortable in their surroundings but then one of them began to feel very unwell. She began to feel extremely hot and her head began to pound. Eventually the pain in her head and dizziness became too much and she lay down on the floor.

Another team member went and sat in the same place where her colleague had begun to feel ill. Again at first, she was fine, but after a few minutes she too began to feel less than comfortable. She was visibly short of breath, almost like asphyxiation. Immediately she moved from the area. Eventually it was agreed that for their safety both team members who were feeling unwell should vacate the area. Once downstairs again, the feelings they were experiencing soon began to dissipate.

So, it was left to the rest of the team to carry on the vigil. Preliminary temperature readings found the room to be at an average temperature to the rest of the building and similar to that of the other flat and downstairs. It was slightly higher but that is a normal occurrence as it is a common scientific fact that heat rises. However, as the team carried out the vigil the temperature began to rise. A small

BELOW *The great hall, one of the most active locations at the Royal Victoria Patriotic Building.*

fluctuation was to be expected as the introduction of body heat would cause the room temperature to increase, but after two members of the team left the room the temperature continued to rise. It was also being felt by the members of the team and everyone found it difficult to acclimatise.

Eventually at the height of the investigation the temperature had increased by 8°C. This was difficult to attribute to any common and natural reason, and it was confirmed by the owner that no form of room heating had been on all day. Also, on further examination of photographs taken at this point it was noted that the velux window was also open allowing any warm air to escape. So why had the room become so hot?

One explanation could be an example of the SWPT. Maybe the distress and reaction felt by these two team members was a result of a forced impression. This area was not far from where the fire that killed the young girl had taken place. Both the afflictions described are commonly associated with smoke inhalation and the rise in temperature could also contribute to this theory. It is a distinct possibility that the sensations experienced were of a paranormal nature. It is something that cannot be completely proven, but neither can it be unproven.

ABOVE Almost every person the team met that night had a different tale to tell about the building and its other inhabitants!

SINGING IN THE CHAPEL

The owner of the flat that the team had just been to also owned office space over the other side of the building. Back outside into the dark night they made their way round to the back of the building. Standing away from the corner of the office entrance was the chapel. It was a very modest structure in comparison to its grand surroundings, but equally attractive. A large stained glass rose window glistened eerily in the fading light.

As the team approached the small chapel one of the members thought they could hear music. At first it was thought that it was caused by a party that was taking place nearby, but she quickly dismissed this, as it didn't sound like modern music. The team all listened carefully but at first all they could hear was the droning beat of pop music.

Adamant that she could hear something much different, she urged the team to stand closer to the chapel. Another member moved across the narrow driveway and gently put their ear up against the wooden door. After a few moments he too began to hear something that sounded more like choir music. It was relatively faint but appeared to emanate from inside the chapel. There was no-one in there and the chapel was securely locked.

Although no answer as to what the ghostly choir music was could be gained at the time, it could not be dismissed as more than one person heard the same thing. Unfortunately, due to the music from the party it was pointless trying to record any footage, as it would be difficult to distinguish any other sounds that may have had a more paranormal origin.

ANOTHER CELLAR, ANOTHER GHOST!

The office was yet again a more modern setting and the team were met with a wealth of up-to-the-minute technical equipment and designer office furniture. Surely not a place for the paranormal?

However, the Haunted Britain team knew better than to dismiss a location simply because it doesn't look haunted. Knowing the history of the building and what it was used for, nothing could be written off and despite the contemporary appearance there was a strange feeling about the room that interested the team.

At first, the team didn't really know where to start. EMF readings were not going to help as there was so much electrical equipment in a very confined space that could not be discounted if any readings were detected. It was also very cramped and not particularly quiet. The owner disappeared

under a desk towards the end of the room. 'Anyone feel like going down there?' he asked.

The team peered behind the desk and saw a small hatch in the floor. Within the hole was a small basement used for storage. Many workers had expressed a particular dislike of this area and often refused if asked to venture down there. Three members decided to take the plunge and lower themselves onto a rickety chair – their only means of entry or indeed exit.

Once in the basement it became clear that this area was not used very much at all. Thick with dirt and gravel the room was less than inviting. It was very long, thin, and particularly short on headroom, making it difficult to stand up. The first thing they had to take into consideration was the amount of dust that could be disturbed. There were also rat traps so this could be a possible cause for any strange noises. With this in mind the team started to move along the narrow room.

It wasn't particularly scary or eerie but it certainly didn't feel comfortable. As the team moved further into the area, they noticed large holes that had been knocked into the walls. There was no light source behind each of the three holes making them decidedly creepy. Shining a torch into one of the holes, it was noticed that there were two further rooms.`

Before any dust could be disturbed in these rooms, a few shots on digital cameras were taken to see if there were any orbs or light anomalies present. Two members then made

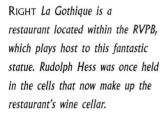

RIGHT *La Gothique is a restaurant located within the RVPB, which plays host to this fantastic statue. Rudolph Hess was once held in the cells that now make up the restaurant's wine cellar.*

their way through into the central room of the basement. Once again it was full of debris. There wasn't a pleasant feeling in this area, but this could be explained by the fact that it was extremely difficult to get out, which gave the members the impression of being particularly vulnerable.

Once in the central room it was discovered that there was yet another part of the basement. It was noticed that the floor in the third room was lower than in the two accessible areas. This was because it had not been used or easily reached for many years.

A camera was set up to film into one of holes in the central room in the hope of someone or something wanting to make contact. Unfortunately after 30 minutes of footage, nothing was captured of any interest.

Even with the lights out, this dark room still didn't feel especially haunted. There wasn't an eeriness or ominous feeling but it was quite oppressive and none of the team members wanted to stay longer than necessary. Surprisingly though, regardless of the lack of atmosphere, two members of the team did experience a strange noise from below the entrance of the basement. As they were talking to each other they both heard a heavy and rough sigh. Neither said anything at first but looked at each other with a rather puzzled expression.

They asked each other what they heard, and both described the same sound. They looked around the room and neither of them could see anything that could make that sort of sound. They also attempted to replicate the sound but nothing they tried sounded like what they had heard. Were they alone? Or was someone trying to make themselves known to the team?

Time at this location was running out and with very little other activity the team decided to vacate the basement and move on. Pictures taken during the vigil revealed a few strange light anomalies – peculiarly these appeared in areas where no-one had entered the atmosphere, so it was less likely to be dust or anything that the team had disturbed. With no exact detail of what these rooms were used for it was difficult to ascertain who could be haunting such an area. But the disembodied sigh was enough to make the team question if they were alone in the basement.

An unexpected visit

The team had all but finished their investigation as residents were tucking themselves up in bed. Not wishing to be a burden or a disturbance the team began to pack up their equipment. The guests from the party that had been taking place in the restaurant had started to leave as the team made their way back to the flat of their host. Just as they were about to head home the manager of the restaurant introduced himself to the team. He had heard about the investigation and was excited by the prospect of the team having a quick look around their premises.

The team had heard a few stories about the restaurant and that some possible paranormal activity could have been to blame for many of them. Even though the team was tired and most of the equipment had been packed away, they gladly took the opportunity.

Inside the restaurant it seemed relatively peaceful, although the atmosphere

LEFT *The team take initial baseline tests before beginning their investigation.*

was still buzzing from the party. Modern gothic décor and detail kept this amazing place true to its surroundings. It was beautiful, but this wasn't where the activity had taken place. The owner then took the team down into the cellar.

A typical cellar for a busy restaurant, it was full of crates, barrels and furniture, but something made the area seem very unnerving. As they entered the back part of the basement the owner informed them of exactly what the cellar area was used for. These were used as prison cells during the Second World War and were often the location for many interrogations of those held there.

Pictures taken as the team walked through the cellars revealed a selection of clear and distinct orbs and light anomalies. However this was not the most compelling evidence found during their brief visit. As the team were walking around the cells a dictaphone was left recording. One particular cell was home to a very prominent figure during its time as a prison. This was where Rudolph Hess was known to have been held before being moved to another institution for his incarceration. As the team were told this, a strange unrecognisable voice was heard on the tape. Although it cannot be completely confirmed, the voice appears to say 'Paul Dixon'.

None of the team know anyone by this name and nor was

SUMMARY OF THE INVESTIGATION

The Royal Victoria Patriotic Building is an amazing and extremely beautiful location. Steeped in history and activity it provided the team with a wealth of emotions and feelings as well as some interesting evidence to support the many claims of paranormal activity that had been reported.

With further investigation, this location could one day reveal more of the secrets of its varied and remarkable past.

he a member of staff or resident at the hall. Further investigation is required as to who this person could be or in what capacity he was attached to the building but it was increasingly apparent that the team had stumbled upon a building that had more residents than they actually knew about.

BELOW *The cellar was used as holding cells during the war. Here we see a strange light anomaly moving across the camera shot.*

THE TALBOT HOTEL
NEW STREET, OUNDLE, NORTHAMPTONSHIRE, PE8 4EA

PREVIOUS SIGHTINGS AND EXPERIENCES

• Taps, bangs and other sounds emanating from the staircase
• The ghost of Mary, Queen of Scots, which has been seen by guests and hotel staff
• Strange noises and cold spots in the two upper rooms

THE LOCATION AND ITS HISTORY

The Talbot Hotel in Oundle, Northamptonshire was formerly known as 'The Tabret', a word that describes a form of tabard, a sleeveless coat worn by heralds. The building was constructed in AD 638 by a group of monks, who built the establishment to provide food, drink and shelter to pilgrims and wayfarers.

In 1626 one William Whitwell rebuilt the Talbot's frontage, using stones from the ruins of nearby Fotheringhay Castle. In 1638 the oak staircase, which once led to the top of the castle in which Mary, Queen of Scots was kept under house arrest until her execution in 1587, was also installed and remains in the hotel to this day. It is said that the ring on

Mary's hand made the outline of a crown in the polished wood of the balustrade, and that it was embedded there as she gripped the rail on her way to the block. The same windows through which Mary looked down onto the preparations for her death, now look out onto the courtyard of the Talbot Hotel. A small gate, which once marked the boundary of Mary's prison confines, divides part of this stairway. She was never allowed beyond it. Some say they have seen the ghost of Mary standing by the staircase window, gazing out defiantly, as she did on that grim morning in February 1587.

It is on record that the executioner who was to behead Mary lodged at the Talbot the night before her death. It is noted that he 'partook of pigeon pie, drank a quart of best ale and made a merry discourse with the serving girl 'til the early hours of the morning'!

The main entrance of the hotel has always been on New Street, formerly Bury Street, and a much-needed right of way through the site was arranged early in its history. The ground was known as Dodd's Yard and in the middle of the 17th century it became famous, as a traveller recorded at the time (see box on the right). Towards the end of the 17th century, this activity diminished, and the well is now filled in, but Dodd's Yard, or Drummingwell Lane as it is called today, still provides the access to the rear of the hotel.

THE INVESTIGATION BEGINS

After a guided tour of the hotel, the team entered the warm and welcoming conference room to set up a base for their studies and to begin their investigation into this famous establishment. The kit was laid on the table and the team discussed which areas needed to be investigated, particularly with regards to the previous sightings at the hotel. It was determined that the first two vigils would take place in the Mary, Queen of Scots and Fotheringhay suites.

The baseline tests were difficult, as a large window stands next to the staircase. The room was a lot colder than the others and seemed to fluctuate around the 22°C mark. However, any cold spots discovered in this room could not be counted because of the large window and the additional ventilation provided for the comfort of the guests.

'There is much discourse of a strange well at Oundle, Northants, in the yard of one Dodd wherein a kind of drumming in a manner of a march is said to be heard; it is said to be very ominous, having been heard heretofore and always precedes some great accident. I wrote to the town for an account of it and was informed of the truth of it, and that it beat for a fortnight the latter end of the last month and the beginning of this and was heard in the very same manner before the late King's death of Cromwell, the King's coming in and the fire of London.'

THE FOTHERINGHAY SUITE

The team entered the lavish Fotheringhay Suite and immediately took up positions around the room, including around the impressive bed and in the main living area. Ten minutes were taken to allow the atmosphere in the room to settle and for the team to focus. Then the investigation into the Talbot Hotel began.

OPPOSITE *The Talbot Hotel is a remarkable building, steeped in history. It is nestled in a small town, which plays host to a staggering number of ghost sightings.*

RIGHT *The rooms of the Talbot Hotel are said to be haunted. Mary, Queen of Scots was held here and some say they have seen her ghost standing by the staircase window, gazing out into the courtyard.*

in the Fotheringhay Suite, so the group decided to move, heading towards the infamous Mary, Queen of Scots Room.

THE MARY, QUEEN OF SCOTS ROOM

The team entered the Mary, Queen of Scots Room with a degree of trepidation, as the room was named after the famous ghost that is said to haunt the Talbot Hotel. It is a ghost that many people have witnessed, both on the main staircase and in the room named for this legendary queen. The atmosphere in the room was very welcoming and with the lights off, this did not seem to change.

With the lights on, this room is beautiful and fit for a king – or queen. However, when the lights are turned off a different feeling overwhelmed the group and the enormity of the task ahead seemed to dawn on everybody present.

The team began with an attempt to communicate with any spirits present. Almost immediately, a member of the group seated in a chair at the back of the room noticed her digital thermometer dropping in temperature. The original baseline measurements of the room had provided a temperature reading of 24°C and the digital thermometer was now reading an impressively low 16°C. This drop of 8°C was recorded in just five to ten seconds and seemed to centre specifically on this chair. The team member in the chair decided it was best to move and the group turned their focus towards the area containing the cold spot.

As questioning began again, the temperature started to increase very slowly, incrementing in 0.1°C steps before finally racing towards the original temperature of 24°C. Could this temperature change have been the result of paranormal activity? The baseline tests had not indicated any unusual cold spots within this room and the group all remained warm, seemingly unaffected by the events.

Questioning continued for approximately an hour, with the group remaining intent on the chair that had been the focus of the cold spot. Unfortunately, after the initial dramatic drop in temperature, nothing else seemed to occur

The team took their positions around the room, some placing themselves in alcoves, others deciding to sit in more open areas. As always, time was taken to allow the room to settle and for the team to focus on its task.

It seems that when you are in a dark room, either alone or with others, the darkness seems to encroach on you and make you more aware of the possibility of strange things happening around you. The Mary, Queen of Scots Room is not like that, instead exuding a sense of calm and well-being as you enter it.

With the atmosphere settled, the group began to ask questions that were specifically aimed at the ill-fated monarch. However, they failed to elicit any form of response, so the questions were opened to any other spirit that might wish to participate in the investigation and make themselves known to the team.

Before the questioning continued, a moment was taken to create some form of psychic protection. Each team member concentrated on a special and safe place, so that any negative energy or spirit would not be able to come through and cause any harm to the group.

The team linked hands, sat around the large table in the middle of the room and the questioning began.

'If there is anybody in the room with us now who wishes to make themselves known, please come forward and try to talk to us. Try in

any way or form that you possibly can, this can be a noise, a light or simply tugging the clothing of any team member you choose.'

Questioning continued in this fashion for around 30 to 45 minutes, but nothing seemed to occur. A locked-off camera had recorded the team for the entire séance and on watching the footage and listening to all audio sources available from the investigation, it was clear that nothing did occur during the investigation into the Mary, Queen of Scots Room.

GOING IT ALONE

The team decided to concentrate on the famous staircase that had been taken from Fotheringhay Castle. However, one member of the group decided to return to the conference room and try to communicate with spirits alone, as through-out the night, one particular spot had stuck in his mind.

As the rest of the team left the room, the door was bolted and readings were taken. The lone member of the team sat against the far wall and after a short period of time,

OPPOSITE The haunted staircase is the most famous feature of the Talbot Hotel. It is said that Mary, Queen of Scots can be seen walking down the stairs towards her execution.

attempted to communicate with whatever may be lurking in the shadows.

'It's OK … it's just you and me.'

There was no response.

'The rest of the team have gone now, so there is no need to be shy.'

Again, no response.

'Please try as hard as you can to talk to me, you can even try to touch me if possible.'

No response.

The room seemed strangely quiet, as if the team member was waiting for something to happen that would be out of the ordinary. However nobody seemed to want to come and say hello!

BELOW The lavish Mary, Queen of Scots Room is home to a number of different paranormal sightings.

After 35 minutes of questioning, with no obvious sign of communication from any form of ghost or spirit, the room was vacated, and the individual joined the rest of the team.

THE STAIRCASE

The famous staircase from Fotheringhay Castle seemed to vanish into the depths of the Talbot Hotel, carrying a sense of omniscience with it. Every member of the team present described the feeling that something was at the top of the staircase watching the entire group conduct the investigation – could this feeling have a paranormal explanation? Or was it simply a case of fear beginning to breed fear?

Team members positioned themselves at varying levels on the staircase and began to ask questions and request some form of acknowledgement from anybody present. Then suddenly – TAP!

The noise set the team aback, as, although half-expected, it seemed to come from the two rooms that had just been investigated. So a member of the group decided to check and ensure that something obvious wasn't creating the noise. Nothing had been discovered that hadn't already been outlined in the baseline tests, so the questioning continued.

'If there is somebody on this staircase with the team, excluding the team members, who wishes to make themselves known, could you please come closer towards us and try to speak to us, you can talk to the machines that we have with us, even though we may not be able to hear you, these machines can.'

Nothing...

'Feel free to use the energy in this room, and within the group. Try and talk to one of the team members, please tell us who you are and why you are here. If that is asking too much then please try and do all that you can. We mean you no harm, and we come with the utmost respect for who you are – all we wish to receive is some form of proof that you are still resident on this staircase.'

Unfortunately, after more than an hour of questions, which were asked by different members of the team, no phenomena were reported, so the team headed back to the meeting room for a debrief. All present firmly agreed that the Talbot Hotel is a fantastic building, steeped in history with some impressive furniture and, although nothing seemed to happen during the investigation, there was a definite feeling that we had not been alone in the hotel.

RIGHT *The staircase was moved from Fotheringhay Castle to the Talbot Hotel where it currently resides. But did it take the ghost with it?*

SUMMARY OF THE INVESTIGATION

The Talbot Hotel is a classic case of an investigation in which things start to appear when you begin to review your evidence. The temperature drop in the Fotheringhay Suite can clearly be seen on camera, as the infrared thermometer continues to drop even though it is directed towards the same spot on the wall. The strange thing about this phenomenon is that the temperature is normally expected to rise slightly when a group of people enter a room – so what caused this drop of 8°C? Could it be paranormal? Unfortunately, the answer to this question seems to be a long way in the distance.

The greatest piece of evidence captured during the investigation into the Talbot Hotel, was discovered while listening to the camcorder's audio track, which was recorded during the lone investigation in the conference room.

As mentioned in the reference section of this book, it is very important to listen to the audio sounds from all camera footage – as countless things could be missed. This piece of evidence is testament to this.

During the lone investigation, the team member was left in the room with the door bolted. The remainder of the team were on the staircase, which is some way away from the door. Tests were undertaken to see if this individual could hear the rest of the team during the vigils, and nothing could be heard through the solid walls and even more solid door that closed the conference room off.

Listening back to the audio, it seems that an EVP was captured that appears to respond directly to the team member's questioning, although in what context we will never know.

The conversation is recounted here, with the EVP also documented.

'It's OK ... it's just you and me.'

No response.

'The rest of the team have gone now, so there is no need to be shy.'

Then an EVP is heard on the tape, saying 'Why?'

'Please try as hard as you can to talk to me, you can even try to touch me if possible.'

Again, an EVP is heard saying, 'Why?'

It seems that some unknown presence had attempted to communicate during this singular investigation. It could not have been any other member of the team or any form of interference on the video camera, as the tape has been analysed for a variety of different defects and none could be found.

This piece of evidence has not been replicated, and there is no explanation as to why it could have happened. All manner of baseline tests have tried to establish a normal reason for this occurrence, and all have failed.

The Talbot Hotel is certainly an interesting building, with the sort of history and furnishings that many prestigious establishments can only dream of. The staircase is a fabulous piece of history that can be seen by all visitors, and sightings of Mary, Queen of Scots continue to this day, a fact that is even mentioned on the hotel's website.

If anything has arisen from our investigation into the Talbot Hotel, it is the fact that all evidence collected has to be examined in every way possible. From tiny pieces of audio to three-hour long tapes that transpire to contain nothing - your next piece of evidence could be languishing on that tape you forgot about!

THE LORD RAGLAN PUB
61 ST MARTIN'S LE GRAND, LONDON, EC1A 4ER

PREVIOUS SIGHTINGS AND EXPERIENCES

- Cold spots experienced in all areas of the pub
- The feeling of being watched
- The sensation of falling or being pushed near the balcony area
- A quivering Roman seen in the cellar

THE LOCATION

Drawn to the hustle and bustle of London, the Haunted Britain team was invited to investigate one of the oldest public houses in the City. Standing on the main road that leads from the Barbican to St Paul's Cathedral, the Lord Raglan has had many names and faces over the centuries, but the pub that is on view today has remained much as it is since 1855. However, the historical significance of the area and the building go much further back in time than the pub's Victorian frontage.

The site of the Lord Raglan stands in an area that was previously occupied by a large Roman fort. Recent excavations of the original Roman city wall have dated some of the foundations below today's city from before AD 130, although the belief is that some areas are even older than that.

ABOVE *The Lord Raglan is one of the oldest public houses in London, and is said to be home to a number of ghosts or spirits. The historical significance of the site dates back to Roman times.*

The Roman invasion of Britain in AD 43 resulted in the creation of the city that is now Britain's capital. Large armies from Rome, led by Aulus Plautius, laid siege to the country. They were met by hostile tribes, determined to defend their island from intruders, but the sheer size of the Roman army made the native Britons relatively easy pickings. Resistance to the Roman invasion gradually dwindled and more tribes conceded to the influence of their invaders.

The Romans' advanced way of thinking and modern understanding of society required them to establish a principle city. With easy access by both road and sea, the strategically placed area known today as London was the first choice. The Romans built a bridge across the Thames and developed an area around it housing military roads and settlements — it was the birth of Londinium.

The city began to grow rapidly and there was an influx of soldiers and native Britons, all of whom needed homes. Houses, municipal buildings, baths, forts and a defending wall were erected to create a formidable and powerful infrastructure.

The fort and defending wall occupied an area of approximately 330 acres. The walls were 18 feet high, 9 feet wide and had trenches that reached 6 feet deep. Each corner of the Roman fort had a defensive tower and in the centre of each spanning wall was a gate. Many parts of the wall still exist, particularly around the Barbican and the Tower of London.

The cellars beneath the Lord Raglan are known to be Roman in origin. During the pub's refurbishment, part of the original Roman walls and possibly even one of the gates were found in the vaults where wine was stored. Subsequent buildings were placed over the original vaults, but care was taken to ensure that not all of the remnants from this significantly important era were removed and destroyed.

Aldersgate, or the fourth gate, stood next to the plot on which the Lord Raglan stands today. It survived well over 1,500 years, but it fell into disrepair and was eventually dismantled when it was deemed beyond restoration. However, surveys of London undertaken in the 16th and 17th centuries have established that a public house was situated to one side of the original Aldersgate.

There can be no doubt that this property has extensive links with London's birth as a city – indeed one of the apparitions seen here is that of a cowering Roman soldier in the basement area. Given the building's obvious link to the Roman occupation of London this is not only interesting but it can be substantiated by historical fact.

The road on which the pub stands is St Martin's Le Grand. From the outside the building appears relatively small in stature, but the interior is surprisingly spacious, with two floors adorned with old wooden and flagstone floors and a wealth of nooks and crannies for more intimate conversation.

Today the area surrounding the Lord Raglan is home to many multinational businesses, colleges, Corporation of London buildings, museums and an abundance of historical and religious properties. Many a weary worker or visiting tourist enjoys partaking in some much-needed liquid refreshment in this warm, friendly and hospitable establishment.

THE HISTORY

The first mention of a public house on the site was in 1530. In those days it was known as the Mermayde, although very little information exists about the tavern from this period. It is thought that it was once frequented by the most famous author, poet and playwright of them all – William Shakespeare. This Mermayde Inn is not to be mistaken with the Mermaid Tavern on Cheapside, which boasts among its historic regulars Christopher Marlowe, Ben Jonson and the aforementioned bard. Some time before the 1600s, the Mermayde became the Bush Tavern. It is thought that this was the building mentioned in John Stow's 1598 Survey of London. He described large Tudor-style houses with diverse room and lodgings around Aldersgate, adding further proof that there has been a building on the site for many centuries.

The Bush Tavern changed its name again after the execution of Charles I in 1649. Emotions and melancholy gripped the city at the untimely death of their king. The capital became a sad and miserable place to live in as monarchy gave way to the rule of a puritanical parliament. However powerful Cromwell and his followers became, the people of London and much of the country were in mourning.

Sensing the depth of feeling, and in response to his own sentiments, the landlord painted the pub's sign black, renaming it the Mourning Bush Tavern. It provided much entertainment, attracting many local businessmen, including the Freemasons and Guildsmen from the local livery companies in the area.

BELOW *The history of the building is displayed for modern day visitors to see and read. The pub has had many different names, but since 1855 has been called the Lord Raglan in commemoration of the great British war hero.*

Anne's Lane, confirming that the inn was much larger than it is today.

Some time before 1739 the pub became the Bush Tavern again. This name remained until 1830, when an extensive refit was undertaken. A new building was erected on top of the original wine vaults of the Bush Tavern, its 6-feet thick walls interlaced with Roman brick. It was completed some years later, and the name changed for the final time in 1855, when the pub became the Lord Raglan, in commemoration of the great British war hero.

LORD RAGLAN

Lord Raglan, or Fitzroy James Henry Somerset, was born in 1788. A well-educated young man, he joined the British forces when he was 16 years old. After just a year's service he had risen to the rank of lieutenant, leading his own troops into battle. The young soldier caught the attention of none other than Sir Arthur Wellesley, Duke of Wellington. He went on to serve him as Military Secretary for many years, and married the duke's niece, Emily.

Raglan fought at the Battle of Waterloo, where he was wounded, losing his right arm. He withdrew from active service and was given a more befitting role as aide-de-camp to the Prince Regent, later George IV. Along with this honour, he was awarded the rank of colonel at the age of 27 and his glorious military career continued. After the death of Wellington in 1852, Raglan was elevated to the rank of Master-General of the Ordnance.

At the outbreak of the Crimean War in 1853, Raglan was chosen as Commander-In-Chief of the British troops, despite the fact that he was 65 years old. He led them at the Battle of Balaclava, and was involved in the infamous Charge of the Light Brigade. The Crimea was not the worthiest war in British history, resulting in calamitous losses and many casualties. The responsibility for this disaster fell heavily on Raglan, and, regardless of his previous successes, he was blamed for the catastrophe.

Raglan continued to serve his country and reluctantly led a daybreak assault on Sebastopol. The British were met with a

The thriving hostelry became a den of gambling, card playing and, more than likely, loose and fancy-free women to provide some 'innocent' entertainment. Like many wealthy establishments, the tavern also attracted its fair share of pickpockets and card-sharks, who singled out the richer punters, relieving them of their hard-earned cash.

After the restoration of the monarchy in 1660, the country began to pull itself back on its feet and the pub's melancholy name was no longer relevant. In 1719 its name was changed for the fourth time when it became The Fountain. Common understanding leads us to believe that this name derived from the existence of a natural spring on the east side of Aldersgate.

Reference to the public house was made in Maitland's History of London in 1722. It was described as The Fountain, although many still referred to it by the previous name. It was also reported that the pub had a back door leading onto St

formidable Russian force and suffered substantial loss of life. Raglan felt ultimately responsible for this failure. Already suffering from dysentery, he fell ill and just ten days into the campaign, on the evening of 28th June 1855, he died. His body was carried back to his beloved England with full military honours. On their way to the port some seven miles of the road from his headquarters was lined with his troops in order to pay their respects to such a great man. He was buried at Badminton nearly a month later and will always be remembered as a decent, loyal and respected war hero.

THE INVESTIGATION BEGINS

The Lord Raglan was not unfamiliar territory for the Haunted Britain team, as they had visited it on numerous occasions in a social capacity. There had always been the sense that something was not quite right about these surroundings on previous visits, and when the opportunity arose to investigate the public house properly the team jumped at the chance.

The group arrived on a bustling and busy Friday evening. The atmosphere was jovial and light-hearted, with many businessmen and women enjoying an end of the week drink.

With so much activity, it was difficult to imagine that there could be a more frightening side to this welcoming and pleasant place.

First impressions of the pub instantly reflect its age and social standing. The ambience and décor are all in keeping with its age and history, with the exception of more modern fittings around the bar area and the fruit machines.

The team was on a tight schedule and time was very limited. It was imperative to get started as soon as possible. With a lot of electrical equipment around the bar area, it was obvious that there would be some very high EMF readings and, sure enough, there were. A baseline sweep was made around the upstairs area and, apart from the area around the bar, nowhere else in the pub recorded any readings of any significance.

A few members of the pub staff remained downstairs and with a balconied area and open staircase, there was no way of stopping the noise escaping upstairs during the investigation. This meant that the team had to be aware that any EVP caught around the balcony could actually be voices from the room below. It was also difficult to isolate all the lights in the building, and much of the investigation had to be undertaken with the lights on. This was an unusual situation for the

OPPOSITE Lord Raglan. He fought at the Battle of Waterloo, was awarded the rank of Colonel at the age of 27 and was chosen as Commander-in-Chief of the British troops at the outbreak of the Crimean War. He died in 1855, a loyal and respected war hero.

BELOW The interior of the pub is in keeping with the age of the building, and its historical background. It is surprisingly spacious, with a large balconied area that looks down over the bar.

Tavern. The tree was removed when the pub was refitted, possibly for safety reasons or to allow more space.

Three members of the team remained in the dining area, while two other members of the team stayed near the balcony. Very quietly they started to ask for anything present to try and make itself known. Digital photographs were taken in the hope that something would show up on the images and a camcorder also recorded the evening's activities. At first, nothing seemed to happen, but the atmosphere gradually started to pick up and some members of the team began to experience strange sensations.

One team member was sitting on a chair in front of a window, through which a cool draught was blowing as it was slightly damaged. However, he began to feel a curious warmth on his back, as if somebody was standing behind him, but there was no heat source anywhere near him. He began to ask if somebody was trying to get his attention. There didn't seem to be any response at the time, but when reviewing the video footage, the team discovered something quite unusual that may explain why nothing seemed to be happening.

Shortly after the team member's feelings of warmth had dissipated, an anomalous voice was heard on the tape saying 'turn that thing off'. The voice spoke in a low whisper, and when the sound was first heard, the team wondered whether it was actually one of them, as it seemed strangely clear. However, the footage clearly showed that the individuals present were too far away from the camera for a whisper by one of them to have been recorded, and nobody appeared to be talking at the time. The person holding the camera was female and the voice heard was definitely male. With no valid explanation available, this proved to be an extremely interesting piece of evidence. Was someone unhappy about the team's presence? It certainly seemed so.

One of the regular paranormal visitors to the pub is a little girl who likes to frequent the area near the games tables. On the night of the investigation, one member of the team, a sensitive, felt the girl's energy as she sat in the corner of the room. The girl wasn't particularly unhappy, but the team member appeared to hear her singing 'Ring-a-ring of roses', a nursery rhyme that evokes the era when plague was rife in London. Although the plague did claim many victims in the city, it doesn't necessarily mean that this little girl was a victim of the disease. There were many illnesses that claimed the lives of young people right up into the 20th century. She could have died from any number of medical conditions — or even in a more sinister way. However, the ghost of the girl wasn't forthcoming with any information, as she was more of a residual haunting (see the Stone Wall Phenomena Theory, pages 23–24) than an actual interactive spirit.

team, but there is no evidence to indicate that paranormal activity only occurs in the dark, in fact if previous experience is anything to go by, it can happen when you least expect it.

THE UPSTAIRS BAR

It was difficult to get any sense of atmosphere with so much light and noise still flooding into the room, but the team did the best they could. There was definitely something in the air, but it didn't feel overly scary or threatening. Everyone remained relatively calm, feeling reasonably comfortable with the surroundings.

From the outside the pub looks like a very small and cramped establishment and once inside the downstairs certainly feels cosy. However, the upper level is wide open and very spacious; a dining area with tables and chairs fills one end, while the other end is dedicated to the casual drinker, with fruit machines and table football. The centrepiece is a large balcony area, which looks over the downstairs bar. The original tavern had a large tree growing through the centre, which is likely to be the reason why it was called the Bush

Now you see him, now you don't...

Throughout the investigation a lot of photographs were taken and a few orbs were detected. It was a difficult situation, as the lighting conditions were causing problems with focus.

One photograph in particular caused a great deal of speculation. A team member was taking some general shots of the area while another member of the team took readings and set up motion detectors. The member with the camera called to him and asked him to pose. He obliged, standing directly in front of the camera and striking a humorous posture.

Laughing at the pose his model had taken, the photographer decided to review the image on the digital screen. You can imagine his surprise when he realized that the subject of the photograph was not visible. At first the team didn't believe that this was possible — perhaps he hadn't actually taken the photograph, even though he believed he had. However, the image displayed the exact scene and it was also the only picture taken of that particular spot. There was also a witness standing next to him as he took the photograph.

Every possible explanation was explored, but the fact remained that the photograph didn't appear to feature its subject. When the team returned to headquar-

ters and looked at the image on a large screen something else exceptional was discovered — a thick white streak of mist was visible right through the centre of the photograph, at exactly the point where the subject should have appeared. The streak seemed to be moving through the table and chairs, but there was still no sign of the team member who had posed for the photograph. What had happened? Why didn't he appear? What does it mean?

RIGHT *One of the team members was in this photograph when it was taken. However when looking at the picture he has disappeared.*

OPPOSITE *The spooky wooden staircase and bar below.*

ABOVE *A host of historical artifacts are placed around the Lord Raglan, could these hold any Stone Wall Phenomana?*

When the image was taken, the pub was practically empty with just the staff downstairs. The upstairs lighting was still turned on, so the photograph should have been fairly easy to take. And it was — until the photographer realized that his subject was not in the image. Everything else was present, although some elements were a little out of focus.

The photograph is bathed in a strange and ethereal orange tint. The lighting is overly bright, as a result of bulbs hanging from the ceiling, which caused a lot of glare and whiteout on certain parts of the photograph. This also shows that the flash was working properly, and all the surfaces are evidently reflecting light, which means that a clear picture could have been taken. But a human also reflects light — so where was the missing team member?

Logic dictates that he was simply not in the frame. However, when camcorder footage of the area was reviewed, it showed quite clearly that he was the subject of the photograph, complete with a silly pose. But is it possible that he moved out of shot just before the still image was taken? This is a likely explanation, and explains why the team member is missing in the final image. Or does it?

There are several known cases in which individuals have taken photographs but their subjects have not come out or have come out incomplete or translucent. Most, but not all, can be explained as double exposures. And what of the urban myth that if you don't appear in a photograph taken of you that you or someone close to you is about to die? Truth or fiction?

Finally, there's the long trail of mist that appears in the image. Perhaps this was tobacco smoke, but if this is the case, why isn't it permeating the whole room, instead localized to a small corridor along the back of the upstairs bar? Could this be a ghost? Perhaps even the very same ghost that also left a very clear EVP calling out for 'Martin'?

We'll leave you to make your own mind up…

TIME TO GO DOWNSTAIRS

Eventually all the staff, with the exception of the owner, vacated the premises, so the team decided to move downstairs into the main bar area. With less noise to contend with, the team finally began to fully experience the pub's extraordinary atmosphere. The lower floor certainly exuded a different feeling from the upstairs.

One area in particular attracted several members of the team. One individual began to experience tightness in her chest, but as she was asthmatic she simply put it down to the general pub conditions. Later in the evening another member of the team sat down in an area that was slightly raised from the main floor and she also described feeling very breathless.

For two people to experience the same discomfort was

unusual, but then a third member came and sat with them. He had been at the other end of the bar, and there is no way he could have heard the other two team members describe their feelings. Within minutes of sitting down in the same area, he found it difficult to breathe. One of the three described feeling as if she was a lot older than her years. It is possible that the feelings that were impressed upon her came from a man who had suffered from a respiratory condition like tuberculosis, or consumption, as it was familiarly known. Then, something changed, the air suddenly became easier to breathe and the three team members began to feel more comfortable again.

It certainly seemed possible that someone was trying to impress their feelings on the team. The area in which the three individuals had been sitting was very open, as it was situated under the balcony. Any cigarette smoke would have filtered through to the upper floors and an extractor fan in the ceiling would have taken it out of the building. Nothing around them could have caused such an instant and obvious change in the atmosphere, the fact that

the feelings also disappeared so suddenly made the event even more intriguing.

Next, one of the female members of the team began to feel as if she was being watched from above. When looking back at the photographs taken at the scene, a small orb is visible on the balcony. The white mist seen on the mysterious picture was also taken in the same area of the balcony that this watchful presence seemed to be standing. The team member who experienced this sensation believed that this person was strong, authoritative and definitely male.

It is possible that this spirit was a former owner or governor of the building, who still used the balcony to keep an eye on his punters. The team member under scrutiny had the impression that this man was something of a crook and liked to rig card games. When she described what she felt to another member of the team, he remarked that he liked to play cards for money and asked if the spirit wanted to come and play cards with him, as he had won a few hands before. The subject of the spirit's attention replied that there was no way her colleague would win – this ghost had ways of making sure!

RIGHT *One of the team members reported seeing a gentleman looking down from this balcony during the investigation. It is thought that he was a previous landlord.*

This was an interesting aspect of the investigation, as at this point nobody had any information about card playing in the pub. Further research after the investigation revealed that the pub was a notorious spot for gamblers and card players in the 18th and 19th centuries. From the clothes and manner the team member had described, this spirit fitted this period well. She also felt that a now-inaccessible room somewhere in the pub was once used for card playing in the 19th century. It is highly possible that the interior of the pub has changed dramatically and the presence of small side rooms or back rooms is more than likely.

As the investigation drew to a close the two female members of the team were mysteriously drawn to the staircase and back to the top floor. One of them had seen a dark shadow ascending the stairs, and, without any prompting, her colleague was suddenly drawn to film the bottom of the stairs. They decided to ask for anyone present to make themselves known. Despite their repeated appeals, no spirits seemed to want to respond to their requests.

MAYBE NEXT TIME

Due to the time constraints, it was impossible for the team to enter the cellars on this occasion. This was a real blow for the team, as this was the one area they were looking forward to investigating.

Many previous occupants of the Lord Raglan have witnessed the figure of a Roman soldier cowering in the corner of the cellar. When approached, he has simply faded and swiftly disappeared. Reports of the sightings have revealed that those who had seen him hadn't been particularly afraid, as the figure seemed to be more distressed than they were.

Given the area's historical background and the fact that Roman architecture and stonework has been discovered in the basement, it is less than surprising that a spirit of this description inhabits the cellar. The current members of staff haven't witnessed anything, but this isn't to say that the spirit doesn't exist, as Haunted Britian have learnt that some people are more open to paranormal experiences than others.

LEFT *Baseline tests were taken at 15 minute intervals to ensure that the team had a steady stream of information to work from.*

It was a real shame that the team didn't get to hold a vigil in the cellar, but we only had access to the location for one and a half hours, which was not long enough to complete an investigation of the entire building. Hopefully, we will be able to return to this location in the future to conduct more experiments and hold a vigil in the area that has made this public house so intriguing to paranormal groups.

THE EVIDENCE

Upon reviewing the evidence that was collected during the short time the team were present at the Lord Raglan, the group was pleasantly surprised. Assessing the feelings and sensations that some team members had experienced, it was agreed that it had been a successful investigation, although a short one.

A few orbs were caught on camera and those that were captured were singular and significant. There wasn't much dust around and many of the images didn't require the use of a flash, so the possibility that they were caused by light refraction or the reflection of airborne particles was minimal.

The team also picked up some interesting EVP. The male voice that was heard saying 'turn that thing off' was a great piece of evidence, as it simply could not be identified as anyone in the group — everyone was either visible on camera or too far away for their voices to be picked up by the microphones.

SUMMARY OF THE INVESTIGATION

To the landlady's knowledge, nobody had undertaken a paranormal investigation at the property for some time, if ever. It was possible that the team's gadgets and equipment had frightened off any spirits present. However, it certainly seemed that the team was not completely alone during its short visit. The orbs, EVP, mysterious photographs and impressed emotions are all significant pieces of interesting phenomena that will be further investigated by Haunted Britain.

Given the chance, the team would like to return to the Lord Raglan to investigate the site further. If such stupendous activity can be picked up in just a few hours, just what will be in store for the team with a little more time on its side?

The other EVP took the team by surprise. The woman's voice saying what is believed to be 'Martin' appears to be located right next to the camera. No cold spots were detected at this scene and nobody heard anything at the time. Nobody in the building was called Martin, and it is difficult for the team to trace the significance of the voice, but was someone trying to contact us? One day we may find out.

RIGHT *Laser trip detectors were used in locations where spirits have been said to be seen walking.*

THE ANCIENT RAM INN,
POTTERS POND, WOTTON–UNDER–EDGE, GLOUCESTERSHIRE

PREVIOUS SIGHTINGS AND EXPERIENCES

- The 'Blue Lady' appearing in a section of the Men's Kitchen
- An unknown lady sitting by the side of the fireplace and well
- A full apparition sitting on the opposite side of the fireplace and well
- The apparition of a bartender in an area of the building that was previously the bar
- The apparition of a cat appearing on the bed in the Witches' Room
- Two monks walking and talking in the Bishop's Room
- A cavalier in the Bishop's Room
- The apparition of a shepherd and his dog in the Bishop's Room
- The sight of a woman hanging in the Bishop's Room
- An unknown face appearing at the side of a wardrobe in the Bishop's Room
- Two highwaymen viewed in the attic bedroom
- Furniture moved by invisible forces
- People being hit, punched and thrown around the building
- The apparition of three young girls in the den
- The owner being pulled out of his bed by an invisible force

THE LOCATION

Many different paranormal events had been witnessed, reported and even photographed during previous investigations at the Ancient Ram Inn, so it's not surprising that it holds the title of the one of the UK's most haunted locations, but it is also a fantastically important historical building, nestled deep in the heart of Gloucestershire.

The Ram dates back to the 12th century, and original deeds written in Norman French go some way to supporting the belief that the hostelry is one of the oldest surviving buildings in the country. The Ram also claims to have the oldest window and ceiling in Britain. However this seemingly tranquil building also has a dark side, and it was for this reason that Haunted Britain decided to investigate here.

The Ram is a unique and widely publicized property that has been the subject of many paranormal shows and appearances on television and in national newspapers. Not only is it classed as one of the oldest inns in the country, but it is also one of the spookiest. Tucked away in the small and beautiful village of Wotton-Under-Edge, the building has attracted a wealth of visitors, intrigued by its gruesome yet fascinating story. Because of the recent increase in interest for the paranormal, the owner of the Ram, which is no longer a working pub, barely has a moment to spare and regularly finds himself opening his door to strangers who feel compelled to look around this amazing building.

So well known are the stories about this building that it has even charmed American ghost enthusiasts, many making a special trip across the pond to see what secrets the old inn has to reveal. This mystifies and amuses the owner, who has lived in the property for over 40 years – he cannot quite believe how interested people have suddenly become in his home.

However, there is a sad side to this story. Unfortunately, the Ram has suffered much over the many years of its existence and nearly every room is falling into some sort of disrepair. Although much has been done to make the property inhabitable, it is amazing that this ancient building is still standing. While every effort has been taken to retain its character and age, the structure of the Ancient Ram Inn is in desperate need of attention. The Norman architecture and medieval doors, windows and fireplaces all need restoration and the roof needs replacing.

It would be a tremendous shame if this building were left to dwindle into ruin, as it has such an incredible history and a prominent place in the hearts of many people, including the individuals that make up the Haunted Britain team. It is truly one of the most fascinating buildings that the group has ever had the pleasure to be invited to visit. Let's just hope that it is still around in the future for others to appreciate.

THE HISTORY

The Ram Inn is reported to have been built on an ancient burial mound, possible dating back to Saxon or Norman times. A ley line links the property to Stonehenge and is thought to be the reason for the ever-present paranormal activity. It shares its 12th-century origins with Ye Olde Trip To Jerusalem, which has boasted the title of 'Oldest Pub in England' for many years. However, it is impossible to ascertain exactly how old the Ram Inn is, or date any property from this time accurately unless it has links to a royal establishment

RIGHT *Various artifacts within the Ancient Ram Inn have been used for some form of satanic worship. The inn is not a place for the faint-hearted, easily spooked or inexperienced ghost hunter and anyone with psychic or spiritual tendencies is advised to exercise extreme caution.*

OPPOSITE *The Ancient Ram Inn is said to be one of the UK's most haunted locations. Not only is it classed as one of the oldest inns in the country, but it is also one of the spookiest.*

LEFT *The Ancient Ram is adorned with various artefacts from various ages, including many religious icons.*

or some other historical significance, for only these places have been well documented.

Many people are believed to have received the hospitality of the inn over the years, from everyday punters to religious dignitaries. However, during recent years, the owner of the Ram Inn, John Humphries, has discovered strange objects that indicate the building has links to the darker side of the paranormal.

During general maintenance to the building Mr Humphries discovered a strange wooden disc buried within the chimney. A small section of this disc had been removed, in the same way you would cut a piece of cheese, and within the disc were the remnants of human clothing and hair. This strange object was used in times past as a form of curse, similar to voodoo. The hair and clothing of the cursed individual were placed into the gap in the object and then set above a fire, where the flames reduced these personal effects to nothing but ashes.

As this happened, the unfortunate victim would begin to feel as though they too were burning, and would eventually die of their 'injuries'. This curious object remains intact and seems to be a key to the strange, dark side of the Ram Inn.

Stories that tell of the Ram Inn's association with witchcraft are likely to be the reason for the inflated interest in the site and its sudden popularity. With the discovery of the various artefacts and a history of possessions and 'devil worship', the pub is shrouded in a cloak of mystery and fear.

It has also been recorded that the Ram was the final resting place for many an unfortunate guest. Only a short while after moving in to the property, Mr Humphries was woken one night by a strange and inexplicable force yanking him by his wrists and pulling him out of his bed. Somewhat disturbed by this, he called in a team of dowsers with divining rods. When they encountered strong reading from one side of the bed, the team suggested that the area be excavated. To their horror, the dig unearthed a grisly find: the skeletal remains of three children were lifted from below the floor, along with a broken dagger. Legend and folklore suggest that such a discovery indicated not so much a murder, but a sacrificial killing. This chilling episode added more speculation to ideas that the pub had once been used by followers of the occult.

With this in mind, Mr Humphries took the step of having the property blessed on several occasions, but it is believed that the sheer volume and strength of the rituals and sacrificial offerings that took place in this building were too strong to completely rid the inn of whatever spirit wishes to reside there. Every doorway, fireplace and window has three clearly marked white circles: a sign that, according to tradition, represents the Holy Trinity — the Father, the Son and the Holy Spirit. The icon is intended to protect those within the building from the entry of witches or their familiars, as the religious connotations warn off any entity or supporter of the devil.

With a ghost around every corner and a story to tantalize anyone with the slightest interest in the paranormal, the Ancient Ram Inn is the ideal location for any serious, dedicated and experienced paranormal investigator. But as a result of the Haunted Britain team's visit, it is highly recommend that you experience some more pleasant and less daunting vigils before you even consider descending on this extremely creepy location. The Ram Inn is not a place for the faint-hearted, easily spooked or inexperienced ghost-hunter and anyone with psychic or spiritual tendencies is advised to exercise extreme caution.

With witnesses to poltergeists and extreme destructive activity, it is commonly thought that this property also hosts an incubus or succubus, a demon that plagues the owner and has even visited guests staying overnight. Do you dare read on?

The incubus or succubus

The most important phenomena to occur at the Ram Inn is that of an incubus or succubus, which resides within the building. In order to explain what has occurred here, we first need to explain what these demonic creatures are.

During the Medieval period incubi and succubi were thought to be demons that harassed the living, and attempted sexual relations with them. Mr Humphries describes the constant feeling of somebody in bed with him, and sometimes experiences eerie hands crawling up his legs when he is lying awake at night. So it seems that at least one otherworldly inhabitant of the Ram Inn could be one of these malevolent spirits. However, there are some important differences to note between the two demons. An incubus is usually male and is thought to lie on sleeping people, usually women, with whom it seeks sexual intercourse. A succubus is usually female and is also thought to attempt sexual intercourse with its victims, however, it favours men.

The existence of these creatures is thought by some to be the result of the general preoccupation with sin in the middle ages. However, a different school of thought suggests that incubi and succubi were created by criminals and rapists to escape punishment. During the infamous witch-hunts of the medieval period, men and women alike were often burned for allegedly having intercourse with demons like those described.

Perhaps the most bizarre legend describes the incubus and succubus as one and the same creature, able to transform into the different sexes at will. A succubus attempting carnal relations with men would collect their semen, transforming into an incubus before using the collected semen on sleeping women to produce demonic offspring.

Could it be possible that such a demon resides within the Ram Inn? Possibly, as there are still cases today that suggest these demons exist. It is reported that every decade a winged creature with talons and bat-like ears swoops over Zanzibar and terrorizes sleeping men. And what about the possibility that alien abductions are carried out by a form of incubus or succubus? We could go on. However, it seems that some of the activity described by Mr Humphries could be related to that of an incubus or succubus. Whatever it is, it certainly gives him sleepless nights and has been responsible for a wealth of surprise attacks on him and his guests.

With this in mind, it was with some trepidation that the Haunted Britain team arrived at the Ram Inn, ready for an overnight investigation.

THE MEN'S KITCHEN

The investigation started with a vigil held in the Men's Kitchen. This is a place where many unsuspecting visitors have seen numerous apparitions with the naked eye. The team stationed themselves around the room, and were very careful not to sit or stand in any spot that had links to any previously reported activity. Camcorders were situated in different sections of the room, and dictaphones were carried by most members of the team. Would anything want to communicate with the group?

Almost as soon as the lights went out, the team noticed how very cold the room became, and a quick temperature reading gave the result of 11°C. It wasn't the warmest of evenings, but the temperature inside was certainly a few degrees colder than it was outdoors. When speaking to John Humphries, he agreed that this was often the case, especially at times when a lot of paranormal activity was witnessed. However, during baseline tests, it was noted that the average room temperature was about the same, so this chilly feeling was definitely not paranormal, just the result of very old stone, draughty windows and a cold night.

Within two seconds of the cameras being turned on, an orb could be seen flying across the shot, before disappearing off screen. It is worth noting that the Ram Inn is a very dusty place indeed and the team were expecting a few problems to be caused by this. However, if the orb was actually a piece of dust, then why were no more caught during the investigation into the Men's Kitchen? It surely follows that a lot of dust would cause a lot of orbs! But this was not the case.

The team allowed the room to settle and took a form of psychic protection – just in case. With so many reports of demonic activity at this location, nothing could be taken for granted and so safety was a paramount issue. After this was done, the team began to ask questions to any spirits that might be present in the room. Unfortunately, no sounds were heard by any member of the team during the investigation.

Oddly, one of the team remarked that she felt extremely cold and kept feeling draughts against her face. Although the room was quite open and the general air temperature was not warm, a check of the team's individual temperatures revealed that she was a staggering 8°C colder than everyone else in the room. With everyone in relatively close proximity, it couldn't be the case that she was sitting in a colder area than every-one else. She was also wearing reasonably thick clothing, but was still shivering. Was this paranormal in origin? It's a possibility. Spirits are known to cause temperature fluctuations and cold spots, and maybe something was trying to impress itself on her. Another explanation is that some people feel the cold more than others, particularly those with less body fat. Unfortunately, the team will never know the true cause.

Other than the strange light anomaly and even stranger fluctuations in the pitch of sounds that were recorded during the vigil in the Men's Kitchen, nothing else transpired, so after approximately an hour, the team decided to move on and enter the Witches' Room.

HUBBLE, BUBBLE, TOIL AND TROUBLE?

The Witches' Room is a strange sight to behold, as it looks like a bedroom from years gone by. However, it has one very strange feature - a large yellow stain on the bed.

It is said that this mark was caused by the ghost of a cat, a witch's familiar, which sits on the bed. It has been seen by many different people, and anyone who has slept here has felt something on top of the sheets. The sheets, unfortunately, have not been analysed for any signs of urine, so the team had to take this strange anomaly at face value and begin the investigation into the strange happenings of the Witches' Room.

OPPOSITE *Heat was of a primary concern for the team as the building is very old, and the temperature was only −2°C at various points throughout the night.*

RIGHT *The cat of a witch is said to lie on this bed. The stain is said to be urine from the cat, and can not be removed.*

Shortly after the vigil began, Mr Humphries gave the entire team a fright when he entered the room suddenly to ask if he could join it. He said that many people had seen or photographed orbs while he and another person shared a chair close to the window and fireplace. One member of the team volunteered to sit in the chair, while Mr Humphries perched himself on the arm. Once both parties acknowledged they were comfortable, questions were asked of any spirit or ghost that inhabited the Witches' Room.

A series of 24 photographs were taken of Mr Humphries and the member of the Haunted Britain team as they sat in the chair, and a strange blue light anomaly was captured on the curtains behind both of them. This orb appeared in photograph number 13, but was not in any of the remaining images. Could this have been something paranormal? Perhaps the ghost of the cat that is said to prowl around the room?

During the vigil in the Witches' Room a strange EMF seemed to develop over the course of a few minutes. The dimensions of the field seemed to be 6-feet long, 2-feet across and 1-foot high — but shortly after it was recorded it simply vanished.

The strange fact remained that this was the only piece of evidence that was caught in the Witches' Room, no other orbs that could be dust, no temperature drops, no EVP — nothing.

The team remained in the room for approximately an hour. The activity surrounding the bed and the fluctuations in EMF appeared to have stopped and, with so much more to be investigated, the group decided to move next door and head into the infamous Bishop's Room.

KNOCK THREE TIMES TO ENTER

During the initial walk around the building, Mr Humphries told the Haunted Britain team of a custom he has adopted whenever he enters the Bishop's Room. Historically, this ritual was followed by any staff who wished to enter the room when an important guest lodged here. A large crook is struck slowly onto a small piece of wood on the door three times, and then the following question is asked.

'Is there anybody there?'

Mr Humphries revealed that many people have heard strange voices coming from the room and have simply not wanted to enter and investigate. A previous visitor was apparently thrown off his feet by a ghostly occupant in this room. However, this wasn't to be the case for the Haunted Britain team.

The crook was taken from its stand, rapped sharply onto the door and the question was asked. Nothing …

We quickly opened the door, and even for a group of hard-nosed investigators like the Haunted Britain team, it was clear that the air was filled with a sense of apprehension. The room was empty and the members of the group took their positions around the perimeter of the room, with one individual sitting on the middle of the three beds. It is significant that all investigators in this room, apart from one, reported feelings of unease and cold. It was the first time the team had felt so peculiarly nervous.

During the initial walk around, one particular area in the Bishop's Room yielded very high EMF readings. It was the area where a lady is said to have been seen hanging from the ceiling. With no obvious or hidden electrical cables or equipment in the area, this was an extremely unusual piece of evidence in itself. Even more substantial, and stranger still, was that the EMF had mysteriously disappeared!

EMF Meters are a great tool for paranormal investigators. However, in ancient buildings with unsafe wiring they can throw you off the scale somewhat, with high readings emitted by wires running through the floor, walls or ceiling. If the EMF around the area where the lady is seen hanging was a product of faulty wiring nearby, the field would remain constant throughout the evening. It would not, indeed could not, suddenly disappear. This only gave more credibility to sightings of the hanging lady.

During the vigil in the Bishop's Room, a total of six orbs were captured on video camera. One was captured on two different camcorders at the same time, and another seemed to split into two separate light anomalies, flying between two members of the team, and disappearing in two different directions.

Again, the Ram Inn is a very dusty place and insects were noticeable during the evening. However, during thorough baseline tests no insects were recorded in the Bishop's Room, and it was kept very clean. This again raises the frequent argument about dust and genuine light anomalies, and the answer is always the same: if the light anomalies were dust, why were only six captured on camera?

The vigil in the Bishop's Room made almost all members of the group extremely cold. The ambient temperature circulated at around 15°C, however, one member of the group reached a jaw-dropping 12°C and was obviously cold, as she was shivering and huddled up on the larger of the three beds. She also described feeling unwell and was on the brink of tears. She couldn't explain these odd sensations, but eventually she had to remove herself from her position on the bed. Shortly after this, she felt her throat tighten and began to cough. Could these emotions have also been linked to the hanging lady? Strangely, it wasn't until she left the room that she began to feel more comfortable again.

Various attempts to communicate were made, while using the dictaphones to try and record any responses, and several strange noises were found when listening to the recordings of the vigil.

Three hums were captured on the tape, each one slightly longer than the previous. They occurred over a very short period of time, and have been analysed using sound-editing equipment to try and detect their frequency. It transpires that they are of a normal human vocal range – however, they do not sound like any member of the team present, and cannot be easily explained as they

do not tie in with any of the episodes reported from the Bishop's Room.

The most impressive EVP, however, happens shortly after a member of the Haunted Britain team talks about the fantastic artefacts within the room. A strange voice, unrecognizable as any of the individuals present, states: 'Now look at this.'

Could this have been a direct response from a spirit or ghost, or could it have been strange sounds that we have interpreted as human voices? Again the sound has been analysed and it is definitely within the human vocal range. When members of the team tried to replicate the noise, there was no match. Mr Humphries was in the other end of the building at the time too, so with everyone accounted for, who was this?

THE ATTIC BEDROOM

When baseline readings were taken in the Attic Bedroom, Mr Humphries told us about an incident that happened to a member of his immediate family. The individual involved was deeply interested in tarot cards and had them stored on their bedside cabinets. One evening, something happened that could not be explained: the bedside cabinets were lifted from the floor, thrown out of the room and down the attic staircase.

The relative reported this to Mr Humphries, the room was investigated and a series of tarot cards were discovered. They

BELOW The Bishop's Room plays host to a staggering six ghosts, although there may be more! It yielded very high EMF readings in the area where a lady is said to have been seen hanging from the ceiling.

were arranged in a perfect circle on the floor of the room, and had not been there before the incident happened.

The attic is more famously known for the ghosts or spirits of two of the last highwaymen in the country, namely Will Crewe and Skuse. The two attempted a daring escape when they were discovered, leaping through a small gap into the Bishop's Room and jumping from the window where they were apprehended by guards. It is said to be the ghosts of these two highwaymen that still reside in the attic today.

Baseline readings taken in the attic were astronomically high. However, a quick look outside provided the team with the information that telephone and electricity wires protruded through the ceiling. Luckily the bed within the room did not have such a high reading and this was used as a base to conduct the vigil.

Shortly after the vigil began, a member of the Haunted Britain team, who was standing with her back to the door, suddenly jumped. When questioned, she revealed that she felt as if she had been pushed from behind. Nobody was standing in the attic space itself, and, almost immediately after this happened, the EMF Meter kicked itself into life on the nearby bed. At no point was the device touched, other than to reset it. Upon reviewing footage of the scene, a small orb or light anomaly is seen flying past the camcorder and resting upon the bed, where it simply vanishes. Could this have been the ghost or spirit of a highwayman pushing past the team member to enter the room? Or could it have simply been a series of strange coincidences?

The EMF Meter lay on the bed, and began ticking away as if it was close to an electrical source. Nobody was near the EMF Meter during this time, and so it was with the advent of this sudden increase in activity that questions were asked.

'If there is anybody present, excluding the four members of the team, could you please use the box on the bed that is making the noise to talk with us. If you wish to answer a question as "yes" then please move closer to the box, if the answer is "no" then please move away.'

'ARE YOU WILL CREWE OR SKUSE?'

The EMF Meter ticked over very gently, giving out a very minor reading. Previous baselines taken on the bed had given the team a baseline reading of zero — so where had this sudden electric field come from, and why did it start happening?

Further questions were asked, and the EMF Meter simply ticked over as if a ghost or spirit was sitting nearby and watching the group. All that can be added is that the fluctuations were anomalous and could have been coming from the realm of the paranormal.

During the investigation into the attic bedroom, the sound pitch on the camcorders and dictaphones started to go up and down at varying intervals. The Haunted Britain team use DVD camcorders, which avoid the possibility of tape wear and such circumstances arising. When using audio cassettes for dictaphones, the team always use fresh tapes and batteries. The audio has been analysed and, although nothing was found when the pitch was returned to normal, it is still a strange phenomena, and one that the team cannot explain. The camcorder was checked after the investigation and was found to be in full working order.

It is worth noting the following things about this pitch anomaly: the tape was checked on the reverse side and the strange variations were not present. If there was a problem with the tape itself then the varying pitch would occur on both sides of the tape. Second, the batteries were fresh out of the packet, and had not drained during the vigil. If this had been the reason for the strange sounds, then the pitch would have decreased only as audio tape slowed down and the batteries had died.

SUMMARY OF THE INVESTIGATION

The Ram Inn is a famous haunted location and rightly so. The Haunted Britain team captured some undeniably strange phenomena, and some that had never been experienced before. With its obvious age and unforgettable beauty, this location is worth seeing just to appreciate its amazing resilience to the passage of time and historical value. The team have no doubt that it has been witness to tempestuous and often fraught times, and, if local legend and hearsay are anything to go by, this could be one of the most culturally significant and spiritually interesting buildings that remain in this country. The Haunted Britain team have never had the opportunity to investigate anywhere like the Ram Inn before and it was a great privilege to be welcomed into such an awe-inspiring property.

However, there are a few words of warning! Do not investigate a site like this alone! Wear a lot of warm clothing, as you won't believe how cold it gets and make sure you have some psychic protection, you may just need it. And please remember that this is someone's home and while you can walk away from anything you may stir up, he may not be able to.

HAUNTED LOCATIONS

Organising a paranormal investigation is an arduous affair with lots of letters and phonecalls, and of course the owner of the property may decline to have their property investigated. We have tried to compile a list of free locations for groups to visit. Please note that some may need permission from the council. And always remember the top ten ghost-hunting tips on page 15!

There is a plethora of haunted locations in Britain, in fact, it has been argued that it is one of the most haunted countries in the world. Gaining access to sites to conduct paranormal investigations is not easy, it can mean a lot of communication between your paranormal investigation group and the venue, and can also cost quite a lot of money.

There are a number of ways that you can gain access to locations. The first is to attend an overnight vigil with a paranormal tour company. These organizations book large locations that would normally cost an awful lot of money to lease individually. The downside of conducting an investigation in this way is that there are inevitably going to be a lot of people on the scene, and an objective scientific investigation will be almost impossible to achieve. The second way to gain access to haunted locations is to write a letter, stating who you are, your intentions and what you plan to do with any evidence or recordings you may find. The following template can be used in such circumstances.

Main Contact Name
Ghost Group Name
Address
Telephone
Fax
Email

To Whom This May Concern

Thank you for taking the time to read this letter. Permit me to introduce myself, I am **[insert name]** and I am a paranormal investigatior with the group **[group name]**.

Whilst conducting our research into haunted locations, we came across your esteemed venue and wondered about the possibility of conducting a paranormal investigation at your property.

The investigation team will consist of **[X]** members (including myself) and we shall be held accountable for all damage **[if you have insurance it is best to state this here]** to any property.

We would require access to your location for a period of three to five hours during the evening or night in order to conduct a series of scientific tests that will try to capture proof of the existence of the paranormal. At no point shall we be intrusive or demanding, and we will be happy to work around you and conduct the investigation at times suited to yourself.

We will make every effort to conduct this investigation away from the view of the public so as not to arouse their interest. We will also inform the local police of our intentions, so as not to arouse any form of suspicion.

If possible, we would also like to visit your venue in the daytime to have a walk around and get our bearings and make notes of anything that could be construed as paranormal. However this is not imperative.

If you require any considerations to be met before an investigation takes place, please contact us as soon as possible so we can make all members of our investigation team aware.

[insert this following section where applicable]

We would invite you to stay with us during this investigation, as your knowledge of the building will prove both fascinating and insightful if we do encounter any form of paranormal activity.

Thank you once again, I hope to hear from you soon

Yours sincerely,

[insert name]
[position in group]
[group name]

N
W   E
S

Hartlepool

Stockton-on-Tees
Darlington   Middlesbrough

Barrow-in-Furness

Harrogate
York

Blackpool

BRADFORD   LEEDS
Blackburn

HULL

Southport
Huddersfield

Crosby

Grimsby

LIVERPOOL
MANCHESTER
Stockport

Chester

SHEFFIELD

Chesterfield   *Pleasley Vale Mills*

Lincoln

Mansfield

STOKE-ON-TRENT

Galleries of Justice

DERBY   NOTTINGHAM

Stafford   Burton upon Trent

Grace Dieu

Shrewsbury

The Talbot Inn

Tamworth   LEICESTER

WOLVERHAMPTON

Peterborough

Norwich   Great Yarmouth

Hinckley

The Talbot Hotel

Lowestoft

BIRMINGHAM

Kidderminster

Solihull   COVENTRY   Corby

Rugby

Worcester

Northampton

Cambridge

Ipswich

Bedford

Milton Keynes

Gloucester   Cheltenham

Colchester

Luton   Stevenage

Clacton-on-Sea

Oxford

Harlow

The Ancient Ram Inn   *Guild Halls*

The Lord Raglan

Southend-on-Sea

CARDIFF

Swindon

BRISTOL

Reading   Slough

Rochester   Margate

Bath

Staines   LONDON

The Royal Victoria Patriotic Building

Maidstone

Basingstoke

Dover

Crawley   Tunbridge Wells

Folkestone

SOUTHAMPTON

Hastings

Worthing   Brighton

Portsmouth   Eastbourne

Bournemouth

SOME NOTABLE HAUNTED LOCATIONS IN BRITAIN

FAIRFIELD HOSPITAL, ARLESEY, BEDFORDSHIRE
Witnesses have reported seeing the ghosts of former patients wandering around the hospital. Some observers have described the ghosts moving objects and smashing windows too.

CORK AND BULL PUB, LUTON, BEDFORDSHIRE
This pub is a place of known poltergeist activity. The entity is known to move tables, shake objects and even throw stools across the room. Witnesses have reported having conversations with this spirit, in response it usually throws objects around the room.

RAF CHICKSANDS, BEDFORDSHIRE
There are rumours of a sealed tunnel at this location. It was sealed because an unknown and violent entity attacked visitors at this historic location. RAF Chicksands was once a priory that housed nuns and monks. There have been reports of a hidden love affair between two of these religious folk, one of whom is rumoured to remain at the site.

WOBURN ABBEY, BEDFORDSHIRE
Woburn Abbey is responsible for many stories of ghosts, including a recent vision of a man in a formal hat who was seen walking through walls.

SOUTH HILL PARK, BRACKNELL, BERKSHIRE
Witnesses have reported many different apparitions at this location, including the sounds of crying and screaming.

BRIGHTSTONE ROAD, BIRMINGHAM
The ghost of a young boy who went missing and was never found has been seen crying at this location.

FOUNTAIN CLOSE, BIRMINGHAM
Witnesses have reported seeing the ghost of an entire family along this road. The mother died during childbirth and the rest of her family died shortly afterwards.

SHERBURNE ROAD, BIRMINGHAM
People have reported seeing an old gentleman wearing a top hat and picking up his papers during early morning.

UNIVERSITY OF BRISTOL, BRISTOL
The apparition of a headless horseman is said to patrol the avenue close by.

CHESTER WALLS, CHESTER, CHESHIRE
Two Roman soldiers, one of whom may be a general, have been seen walking along the wall at night.

MARBURY COUNTRY PARK, NORTHWICH, CHESHIRE
This location is reported to be haunted by a grey lady.

NEWTON LAKE, NEWTON, CUMBRIA
A white lady is said to haunt the lake, and has been seen on a number of different occasions. She is reported to be the ghost of a woman who was killed by her husband.

HERMITS' WOOD, ILKESTON, DERBYSHIRE
The woods are haunted by a monk who committed suicide many years ago. People have also reported loud noises and feelings of being watched.

POMEGRANATE THEATRE, CHESTERFIELD, DERBYSHIRE
There have been many sightings here of an old lady, who is said to move objects around the room. She is said to be from the Victorian era, dressed in grey and mourning for her lost love. There has also been a sighting of George Stevenson, railway pioneer and father of Robert, walking proudly across the stage.

CITY CENTRE, DERBY
Many different reports of ghostly children in ragged clothing.

WINNATS PASS, DERBY
Legend tells of a young couple in love, but not able to marry, as their families objected to the union. They eloped, setting off along Winnats Pass. Along the way three people jumped them, took their money and killed them. People still hear the cries of the unfortunate victims to this day.

POWDERHAM CASTLE, DEVON
If you wait at the gates of the castle until midnight you may see a sight many have seen before you — a blue-grey mist that seems to morph into a person of small stature.

BADBURY RINGS, DORSET
This ancient hill fort has witnessed many bizarre paranormal phenomena, including a small human-like creature leaning into visitors' cars, an ethereal woman in a black dress and a large dog that runs in front of cars.

CANEWDON, ESSEX

This village is said to be haunted by witches and their familiars. It is also reported that ghostly police erect roadblocks to stop outsiders coming into the village.

OVER COURT, ALMONDSBURY, GLOUCESTERSHIRE

The infamous white lady of Over Court has been witnessed in both the grounds and a lane next to the building. Witnesses have reported seeing a wound on her body. She was killed by her husband, who found out she was having an affair. She dragged herself into the water where she died.

THE ANCIENT RAM INN, POTTERS POND, WOTTON-UNDER-EDGE, GLOUCESTERSHIRE (see pages 142–149)

BLUEBERRY HILL, MAIDSTONE, KENT

The figure of a young woman has been seen in this location, following a horrific car accident. She is said to appear in the middle of the road.

HALL PLACE, BEXLEY, KENT

Seven hundred years ago Hall Place was the residence of one Sir Thomas Atte-Hall. Thomas was killed by a stag in the gardens. His distraught wife threw herself from the tower and her ghost has been seen at the site. The buildings are currently in the hands of Bexley Council and are open to the public at any reasonable time.

NIGHTCLUB (NAME UNKNOWN), ROCHDALE, LANCS

It is reported that two people decided to dance on the rooftops, lost their balance and fell to their untimely deaths below. Passers by have reported seeing the dancing figures from time to time.

THE STORK HOTEL, BILLINGE, LANCASHIRE

The crypt beneath the current building is said to have been the location where a cavalier met his torturous end. The hotel is also haunted by a highwayman named John Lyon.

GRACE DIEU PRIORY, THRINGSTONE, LEICESTERSHIRE (see pages 96–103)

THE TALBOT INN, 4 THURCASTON ROAD, LEICESTER, LE4 5PF (see pages 78–87)

THE LORD RAGLAN PUB, 61 ST MARTIN'S LE GRAND, LONDON EC1A 4ER (see pages 132–141)

THE ROYAL VICTORIA PATRIOTIC BUILDING, FITZHUGH GROVE, TRINITY ROAD, LONDON SW18 3SX (see pages 114–123)

ST JAMES'S PARK, LONDON

The headless apparition of a monk has been seen at this location on many occasions.

WHITECHAPEL, LONDON

The ghostly form of Polly Nichols, the first victim of Jack the Ripper, is said to haunt this location.

THE TALBOT HOTEL, NEW STREET, OUNDLE, NORTHAMPTONSHIRE PE8 4EA (see pages 124–131)

BLOODY BUSH ROAD, KIELDER, NORTHUMBERLAND

Willowbog Cottage lies on this historic road, and every bridge built at this location has collapsed inexplicably. After one bridge was demolished, it is said that the stonework was covered in blood.

THE GALLERIES OF JUSTICE, HIGH PAVEMENT, THE LACE MARKET, NOTTINGHAM, NOTTINGHAMSHIRE NG1 1HN (see pages 88–95)

PLEASLEY VALE MILLS, OUTGANG LANE, MANSFIELD, NOTTINGHAMSHIRE NG19 8RL (see pages 104–113)

PUBLIC PARK, PAULTON, SOMERSET

An old lady is said to sit on one of the park benches. She has been heard to say 'Have you seen my daughter, she was here last night?'.

PRESTON PARK, STOCKTON ON TEES

A small dog has been seen in the grounds of the park, close to the bandstand. It is also said to run through walls.

WINDMILL CLOSE, LITCHFIELD, STAFFORDSHIRE

Witnesses have reported a 'dark' and 'disturbing' man walking the streets late at night. However, these reports have always come from children. The local papers have been informed, but have ignored the subject, according to reports.

HORSELL WOODS, WOKING, SURREY

Witnesses have reported seeing a young male gliding through the woods.

THE PRIORY, GUISBOROUGH, TEESIDE

The priory grounds are said to be haunted by the ghost of a monk.

DEAD MAN'S GULLY, CARDIFF, WALES

Tales are told of a man who committed suicide in this infamous gully at 10pm at night. Various people have witnessed a paranormal re-enactment of this event.

ETTINGTON PARK, ALDERMINSTER, WARWICKSHIRE

The famous grey lady of Ettington Park is one of the few ghosts to have been captured on a photograph. Many people have also reported the sounds of children screaming coming from the river – the same river in which a child drowned during the 18th century.

GUYS CLIFF, WARWICK, WARWICKSHIRE

Legend tells of a young boy, whose fingers were cut off for being kind. The child still wanders the grounds in pain.

MAIN ROAD, DEVIZES, WILTSHIRE

People have reported seeing a highwayman along the main road.

THE RED LION PUB, AVEBURY, WILTSHIRE

The Red Lion is said to be haunted by a young woman by the name of Florrie. She died after being cast down the well by her husband, who had discovered she was having an affair. Many people have described the sensation of fingers running through their hair.

DELANEY HALL, BARNSLEY, YORKSHIRE

Delaney Hall was once a maternity hospital and workhouse. People have reported the sounds of children crying, the apparition of a young girl called Sally and an old lady with grey hair. Witnesses have also felt very intimidated by the hall and experienced strange, eerie feelings throughout the venue.

STOCKBRIDGE BYPASS, SHEFFIELD, YORKSHIRE

Said by some to be one of the most haunted locations in Britain, a young girl has been seen in the middle of the road here, causing cars to crash. There is also a report of a very angry monk who has been seen hitting vehicles.

THANKS, ACKNOWLEDGEMENTS AND REFERENCES

With sincere thanks:

The owners, staff and regulars of The Talbot Inn, Leicester
The staff at The Galleries Of Justice, Nottingham
John Humphries, Owner of the Ancient Ram Inn, Wotton-Under-Edge
Sue and Mick, founders of Rupert Mole, Pleasley Vale Mills, Mansfield
The Beadle, Court, Council and members of the Worshipful Guild of Barbers Surgeons
The Beadle, Court, Council and members of the Worshipful Guild of Saddlers
The Beadle, Court, Council and members of the Worshipful Guild of Pewterers
The members of the Trust responsible for Grace Dieu Priory, Leicestershire
The owners and staff at The Talbot Hotel, Oundle
The owners, residents and staff at the Royal Victoria Patriotic Building, Wandsworth
The owners and staff at The Lord Raglan Public House, London
Phil Whyman, Charlotte Drew and the team at www.deadhauntednights.com
Richard Jones
Richard Clarke, Lucy Horrobin and the Trent FM Ghost Hunt team
Rae and Kev at Leicester Sound FM
Clare Nazir and the Outside Broadcast team at GMTV
All of the families and friends of the Haunted Britain Team for their ongoing support, and believing in us even if they don't believe in what we do!

We acknowledge the following people and organisations:

Prism
Nottinghamshire County Council
Leicestershire County Council
Leicester Mercury
Nottingham Evening Post
Toms Gadgets

We are grateful to www.istockphoto.com for permitting us use of the images on the following pages: 5, 41, 44.